Dickens and the Scandalmongers

ESSAYS IN CRITICISM

DICKENS
AND THE

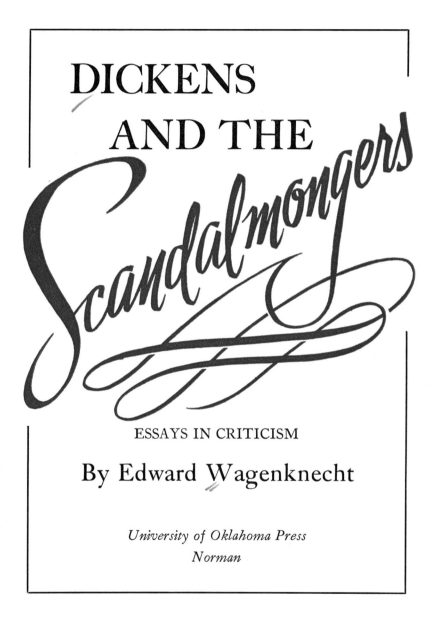

ESSAYS IN CRITICISM

By Edward Wagenknecht

University of Oklahoma Press
Norman

8807

Recent Books by Edward Wagenknecht

Longfellow: A Full-Length Portrait (New York, 1955)
Mrs. Longfellow: Selected Letters and Journals (New York, 1956)
The Seven Worlds of Theodore Roosevelt (New York, 1958)
Nathaniel Hawthorne, Man and Writer (New York, 1961)
Mark Twain, The Man and His Work (Norman, 1961)
Washington Irving: Moderation Displayed (New York, 1962)
The Movies in the Age of Innocence (Norman, 1962)
Edgar Allan Poe, The Man Behind the Legend (New York, 1963)
Chicago (Norman, 1964)
Seven Daughters of the Theater (Norman, 1964)
Harriet Beecher Stowe: The Known and the Unknown
(New York, 1965)
Dickens and the Scandalmongers: Essays in Criticism
(Norman, 1965)

Library of Congress Catalog Card Number: 65–14802

Copyright 1965 by the University of Oklahoma Press, Publishing Division of the University. Composed and printed at Norman, Oklahoma, U.S.A., by the University of Oklahoma Press. First edition.

Preface

IN ITS PRESENT FORM, "Dickens and the Scandalmongers" is new, but it includes vestiges, for the most part considerably reworked, of an identically entitled paper which appeared in *College English* in 1950 and also from a letter entitled "Ellen Ternan," which was published later in *The Dickensian*. The editor of *The Dickensian*, my friend Mr. Leslie C. Staples, has done me the service of reading my paper in a semifinal form and of submitting it, at my request, for critical consideration, to a number of British writers and scholars well versed in Dickensiana. I am grateful to all these persons, but the subject being so controversial as it is, it does not seem to me that I ought to give the appearance of trying to bolster myself by listing their names here and thus perhaps creating the impression that I wish to impute my opinions to them. As a matter of fact, some of them see eye to eye with me while others do not, but I owe it to myself to state that no one of them was able to fault me on any factual point.

The volume in hand is scheduled for publication in the summer of 1965. Shortly thereafter the University of Oklahoma Press plans to publish a thoroughly revised and updated edition of my 1929 book, *The Man Charles Dickens*, which attempts a general study of Dickens's character and personality. Because of the controversy it has occasioned and the biographical problems involved, it was judged best to treat the particular aspect of his experience with which "Dickens and the Scandalmongers" deals separately in this volume; in *The Man Charles Dickens* it will be a properly subordinate part of a larger picture, and those who desire to examine the evidence upon which the writer's conclusions rest can be referred to the present volume. To include this material in *The Man Charles Dickens* itself would, unfortunately, have thrown the whole portrait out of its proper balance.

The introductions to *A Tale of Two Cities* and *Great Expectations* were written for the editions of these novels published by The Modern Library and Washington Square Press, and the essay on *The Chimes* appeared in 1931 in the edition of that work illustrated by Arthur Rackham and published by the Limited Editions Club. The note on Dickens and Ellen Glasgow appeared in *Boston University Studies in English* while I was its editor. The review of the Edmund Wilson book is from *Modern Language Quarterly*, that of the T. A. Jackson volume from the Seattle *Post-Intelligencer*. The excerpts from Katherine Mansfield's *Letters*, copyrighted stories, and *Journal* are used by permission of her publisher, Alfred A. Knopf, Inc. Everything else is from *The Dickensian*, and practically everything contained between these covers has been more or less revised.

EDWARD WAGENKNECHT

March 13, 1965

Contents

Dickens and the Scandalmongers

ESSAYS IN CRITICISM

Dickens and
the Scandalmongers

"You must not tell us what the soldier, or any other man, said,
Sir," interposed the judge, "it's not evidence."

The Pickwick Papers

I

"MEN HAVE DIED FROM TIME TO TIME," says Rosalind, "and
worms have eaten them, but not for love." It would probably be
an exaggeration to say that Charles Dickens died for love, though
it is not unlikely that his crushing sense of "one happiness I have
missed and one friend and companion I have never made" contributed importantly to the suicidal intensity with which he drove
himself through his last years. But even if it is true that Ellen
Ternan made him happy at the end, one must still say that, view-
ing his life as a whole, he can only be described as an unfortunate
lover. He gave the devotion of his youth to a silly girl named
Maria Beadnell, who rejected him. He married an estimable
woman who was in almost every conceivable respect eminently
unfitted to live with him—as he with her—and after many years
they separated. And for a long time that was all the world thought
it knew about his amatory experiences.

During the last generation his biographers and critics have
been assuming that they know much more. But let us see.

Since 1934 Ellen Lawless Ternan (1839–1914) has become
one of the leading characters in the Victorian literary mythology.
She is always spoken of as an actress, and that is what she was, to
the extent that she came of a theatrical family[1] and herself made a

---

[1] See the authoritative account of "The Theatrical Ternans" by Malcolm

3

stage debut at the age of three, but she seems to have had less interest in the theater, and less talent for it, than her mother (an actress of distinction) or either of her sisters,[2] and it is not surprising that she should have left the boards at twenty. Actually she seems to have had much more of the teacher's temperament, and it is not surprising that she should have spent much of her life as assistant to her clerical-schoolmaster husband, George Wharton Robinson, whom she married in 1876. But since we still have with us that particular variety of vulgar mind which finds it easier to credit scandal of an actress than of a woman engaged in any other profession, it would be hopeless to try to get this form of reference changed.

It has long been known that Ellen Ternan and her sister Maria acted with Dickens in *The Frozen Deep* in 1857, that a friendship developed between Dickens and Ellen, and that he left her £1,000 in his will. It has generally been assumed also that it was she whom Dickens sought to protect when, at the time of his separation from his wife in 1858, Mrs. Dickens's mother and sister made allegations which he forced them publicly to retract. This was when he declared that

> two wicked persons who should have spoken very differently of me in consideration of earned respect and gratitude [had] . . . coupled with this separation the name of a young lady for whom I have a great attachment. . . . Upon my soul and honor, there is not on this earth a more virtuous and spotless creature than that

Morley, *Dickensian*, Vol. LIV (1958), 38–43, 95–106, 155–63; Vol. LV (1959), 36–44, 109–17, 159–68; Vol. LVI (1960), 41–49, 76–83, 153–57; Vol. LVI (1961), 29–35.

[2] Her father, Thomas Lawless Ternan, was also an actor and theater manager but apparently less talented than his wife. He committed suicide, insane, in 1846.

young lady. I know her to be innocent and pure, and as good as
my own dear daughters.

He added that "all the late whispered rumors" concerning his
marital difficulties were "abominably false" and that whosoever
should repeat one of them thereafter would "lie as wilfully and
foully as it is possible for any false witness to lie, before heaven
and earth."

Even Dickens' friends have often criticized him severely for
issuing the public statement about his domestic troubles from
which I have quoted, and even more for writing the so-called
"violated letter" which he gave Arthur Smith to show at his dis-
cretion and which found its way into the New York *Tribune* and
was copied elsewhere. Thanks to the researches of Dr. Kenneth J.
Fielding,[3] this point of view now seems untenable, and though we
may still argue that Dickens in 1858 behaved like a man beside
himself, at least we must admit that the gossip which was being
circulated was so much more vicious and widespread than was once
supposed that no decent man could have been expected to permit
it to go its way unchallenged. Newton Crosland, in an insulting
letter, wrote Dickens that the rumors were to be heard "at the
corner of every street & in every social circle." It should not be
forgotten that before acting, Dickens submitted his proposed statement to so knowledgeable a man as John Delane, editor of the

[3] See his "Charles Dickens and Colin Rae Brown," *Nineteenth Century
Fiction*, Vol. VII (1952), 103–10; "Dickens and the Hogarth Scandal," *Nine-
teenth Century Fiction*, Vol. X (1955), 64–74; "The Recent Reviews: Dickens
in 1858," *Dickensian*, Vol. LII (1955), 25–32. The statement from Newton
Crosland, quoted below, is from another article by Fielding, "Dickens and the
Royal Literary Fund, 1858," *Review of English Studies*, Vol. VI (1955),
383–94. See, further, his "Dickens and Miss Burdett-Coutts: The Last Phase,"
Dickensian, Vol. LVII (1961), 97–105.

London *Times*, and that Delane advised him to release it. For the gossip was directed not only against Dickens and Ellen Ternan but also against his sister-in-law Georgina Hogarth, who broke with her family to remain in his house and care for his children (he consistently maintained that it was she, not their mother, who had always done this, and that they would have been lost without her), and it went the length of insinuating not only that there had been criminal intercourse between Dickens and Georgina (which would have been incest by Church of England standards in 1858) but even that this intercourse had produced children. Whether he was right or wrong about it, Dickens believed that the Hogarths themselves were responsible for this monstrous slander, and though he specifically exempted his estranged wife from all suspicion of complicity, he broke off all negotiations for a financial settlement until they had signed the retraction he prepared for them. When they offered to issue a statement exonerating Georgina alone, he refused it on the ground that in view of "the digusting and horrible nature" of the slanders, he did not "think it desirable that [they] should be written down even for purposes of denial." What he demanded and got from his mother-in-law and her daughter Helen was a declaration that

> It having been stated to us that in reference to the differences which have resulted in the separation of Mr. and Mrs. Charles Dickens, certain statements have been circulated that such differences are occasioned by circumstances deeply affecting the moral character of Mr. Dickens and compromising the reputation and good name of others, we solemnly declare that we now disbelieve such statements. We know that they are not believed by Mrs. Dickens, and we pledge ourselves on all occasions to contradict them, as entirely destitute of foundation.

6

In view of the disturbance this gossip created at the time, it seems surprising that so little attention should have been paid to it by writers about Dickens until it was revived in the 1930's. From time to time it was whispered that somebody or other knew something about the cause of the Dickens marital smashup which he did not choose to reveal, but nobody seemed greatly interested in it. In the early twentieth century there was nothing much except the gossipy reminiscences of the journalist John Bigelow, in his *Recollections of an Active Life*,[4] and Bigelow knew so little that he called Ellen Ternan Teman and gave her mother's maiden name as Jarmain instead of Jarman. To the best of my knowledge, the earliest biographer to mention Ellen's name was Ralph Straus in his *Charles Dickens: A Biography from New Sources*,[5] but Straus did not even suggest that the relationship between Dickens and Ellen was ever other than innocent. Neither, for that matter, did C. E. Bechhofer-Roberts ("Ephesian"), who, that same year, published a very bad biographical novel about Dickens called *This Side Idolatry*,[6] and this is the more surprising since Bechhofer-Roberts clearly loathed Dickens personally and presented him as a kind of Pecksniff.

II

The Ternan scandal, as we know it today, began on April 3, 1934, when Thomas Wright published an article in the London *Daily Express*. The next year he repeated his charges, in a modified form, in a notoriously incompetent *Life of Charles Dickens*.[7] Hugh

[4] (Baker and Taylor, 1909–13).
[5] (Cosmopolitan Book Corporation, 1928).
[6] (Bobbs-Merrill, 1928).
[7] (Herbert Jenkins).

Kingsmill promptly seized upon Wright's accusations and accepted them in his biography of Dickens, *The Sentimental Journey*, also published in 1935,[8] a considerably more readable and widely circulated book than Wright's.

What, now, did Thomas Wright have to add to what had hitherto been known or believed?

Wright did not doubt that Dickens's statement about Ellen Ternan was true at the time it was made. But "no great while after," he "prevailed upon Miss Ternan to become his mistress." She "gave herself reluctantly" and for greed of gold. In her mother's name, Dickens took a house for her in Houghton Place, and here "he visited her two or three times a week." On Sunday nights the composer Francesco Berger was often invited, and Mrs. Ternan would also be present. Then the two women and the two men would play cards together, or Berger might play the piano while Dickens and Ellen sang duets, none of which, it may be added, sounds like a desperately dissipated form of entertainment.

This much, with the addendum to be noted hereinafter, was the First Act. The Second Act took place four years later, when one Gladys Storey published in London a book called *Dickens and Daughter*,[9] in which she sought to place the posthumous authority of Dickens's younger daughter, Kate Perugini, behind the Ternan scandal. According to Miss Storey, Dickens made no secret of his love for Ellen, forced his wife to visit her, and drove on relentlessly toward the destruction of his marriage. In May, 1869, she came to Gad's Hill "to stay," whatever that may mean. (This is on pages 127–28; on page 137 she is fetched to Gad's Hill after Dickens's fatal seizure.) Moreover, she bore him a child, a son,

[8] (Morrow).
[9] (Frederick Muller).

8

who died in infancy.[10] The last time his daughter talked with Dickens he wished he had been a better father and a better man. He was, as a matter of fact, "a very wicked man," and after his wife's departure from Gad's Hill he behaved so "like a madman" that his daughter married Charles Collins, whom she did not love, to get away from him.

Before we attempt anything in the way of a critical examination of these views, let us try to see, briefly, how they were received.

III

Edmund Wilson has the distinction of being the earliest critic of note to swallow the Wright-Storey thesis, hook, line, and sinker. This was in his now famous essay, "Dickens: The Two Scrooges."[11] I am far from denying that this was a brilliant, though, as I think, frequently wrongheaded, piece of work; it may fairly be said to have inaugurated a new era in Dickens criticism. Nevertheless it is irresponsible both as criticism and as historical scholarship, and some of its conclusions are vitiated by an ignorance concerning

[10] In the controversy occasioned by the publication of his charges against Dickens, Wright had already asserted, in letters to J. W. T. Ley and Walter Dexter, that "*there were children.*" See *Dickensian*, Vol. XXXIII (1936), 48–49, 51. With Miss Storey "*children*" shrinks to "child," which does not tend to increase the reader's confidence, but rather recalls the unmarried wet-nurse of *Mr. Midshipman Easy* who, rebuked for having borne a child, curtsies and replies, "If you please, ma'am, it was a very little one." See Ley's articles in *The Dickensian*: "Dickens and His Wife," Vol. XXXI (1935), 226–30; "What the Soldier Said," Vol. XXXII (1935), 15–21; "More of What the Soldier Said," Vol. XXXIII (1936), 47–51; "The Double Tragedy of Mary Hogarth," Vol. XXXIII (1937), 205–11; "Father and Daughter," Vol. XXXV (1939), 250–53.

[11] In *The Wound and the Bow: Seven Studies in Literature* (Houghton Mifflin, 1941).

9

Victorian novel backgrounds which nobody should attempt to write about Dickens without first having remedied. Some of these matters are specified in the separate discussion of Mr. Wilson as a critic of Dickens elsewhere in this volume.

The next witness is Professor Lionel Stevenson, writing on "Dickens's Dark Novels, 1851–1857":[12] "In April, 1857, he [Dickens] met and fell violently in love with eighteen-year-old Ellen Ternan, and a year later he officially separated from his wife and installed Miss Ternan in her stead." (Note the delightful ambiguity of the last six words. Did Ellen become the chatelaine of Gad's Hill?)

In 1945–46 Dame Una Pope-Hennessy published the first full-length biography of Dickens to be written since the large collection of his letters in "The Nonesuch Dickens" was made available in 1928.[13] She accepted the Ternan scandal in all its ramifications, referring to both Wright and Miss Storey, though one statement in a footnote on page 401 of the American edition, would seem to indicate that she considered Miss Storey the more reliable witness: "In telling the story I have relied not on Mr. Wright but on the information supplied by Dickens's own daughter, Mrs. Perugini." As we shall see, this is a highly unfair and misleading form of reference.

In 1948 Mr. W. Somerset Maugham, having announced that he would write no more novels of his own, generously and unselfishly took upon himself (for a consideration) the task of cutting and editing some of the great novels of the world, in order that they might be presented to modern readers in what would presumably have been their original form if only their authors had

[12] *Sewanee Review*, Vol. LI (1943), 398–409.
[13] *Charles Dickens* (Howell, Soskin).

had him to advise them in the first place. *David Copperfield* being one of the novels to profit by these blessed ministrations, it was republished in its improved form, in a format designed to appeal to young readers, and with an introduction by Mr. Maugham which had previously appeared in *The Atlantic Monthly*. In its discussion of the Ternan scandal, this introduction can only be described as generously eclectic. For good measure, Mr. Maugham also managed to drag into print, for the first time, so far as I am aware, the hitherto word-of-mouth-circulated gossip to the effect that Mrs. Dickens "drank,"[14] and also to revive the old gossip about Georgina. On this last point, however, he was characteristically magnanimous. "It is very probably true," he pontificated, "that Dickens had no sexual relations with Miss Hogarth."[15]

The year 1949 was a banner year for the anti-Dickensites. First there was Hesketh Pearson's *Dickens: His Character,*

[14] Though I heard this story as far back as 1928, I have never believed it nor heard anything to confirm it, though there is an interesting entry in the diary of Mrs. James T. Fields in the Massachusetts Historical Society, under date of January 4, 1868: "He [Dickens] told J [James T. Fields] yesterday in walking that nine out of ten cases of disagreement in marriage came from drink he believed." She adds, "He is a man who has suffered evidently." Mrs. Fields evidently knew something about Ellen Ternan and sympathized with Dickens. In another entry in her diary Kate is quoted as saying that "her mother did not drink but she is heavy and unregardful of her children and jealous of her husband." (See Arthur A. Adrian, *Georgina Hogarth and the Dickens Circle* [Oxford University Press, 1957], 111.) According to Dickens, his wife was furiously jealous of every woman with whom he came in contact. We have a good deal of information concerning her jealousy of Mrs. La Rue, whom he tried to cure of a nervous or hysterical affliction through hypnotism but in whom he demonstrably had no sexual interest whatever.

[15] Maugham's edition of *David Copperfield* was published by Doubleday. The best account of Georgina Hogarth is in the book by Arthur Adrian cited above.

Comedy, and Career,[16] a considerably more "popular" and more highly embroidered biography than Pope-Hennessy's. And here it was all over again and all stated as established fact: Dickens fell in love with Ellen in 1857, and from that moment his wife's fate was sealed. Ellen did not love him; indeed "the thought of intimacy with him repelled her." But she "could, no doubt, especially when she was having a good time, play up to him so well that he was able to persuade himself of her love." (What would a biographer do without "no doubt"?)

In 1949 Clifton Fadiman accepted Wright-Storey in his introduction to Simon and Schuster's "Inner Sanctum Edition" of *The Pickwick Papers*, magnificently illustrated by Frederick Banberry;[17] Jack Lindsay published an article on *A Tale of Two Cities*[18] in which we were given a foretaste of the curious amalgam of Freud and Marx in which, next year, he was to blast "the great lie" that Dickens led a decent life;[19] finally, a scholar of high repu-

[16] (Harper). For a review pointing out Pearson's shortcomings, though not unmindful of his merits as a writer, see T. W. Hill in *The Dickensian*, Vol. XLVI (1949), 23–30. Donal O'Sullivan, "Charles Dickens: His Biographers and His Times," *Studies: An Irish Quarterly Review*, Vol. XXXIX (1950), 141–53, has excellent discriminating and cogent comment on both Pearson and Jack Lindsay. I am not sure that Pearson's book is, as a whole, more unreliable than Pope-Hennessy's, but I get the impression that her inaccuracies are due to carelessness and blundering, while Pearson frankly calls the imagination to his aid.

[17] In this introduction, Mr. Fadiman also describes Dickens's biographer John Forster as his son-in-law, a blunder which I can only explain on the assumption that he remembered that Scott's biographer Lockhart was *his* son-in-law and that, like Little Buttercup, he "mixed those children up."

[18] *Life and Letters*, Vol. LXII (1949), 191–204.

[19] *Charles Dickens, A Biographical and Critical Study* (Andrew Dakers, Ltd., 1950). Dickens, says Mr. Lindsay, "was determined to end his marriage and seduce Ellen," and he adds, "so much we know from his own statement." He should quote the statement; it would be an interesting addition to Dickensian

tation, Professor Franklin P. Rolfe, published[20] a letter which unquestionably proves that Dickens paid for the Italian musical education of Ellen's sister Fanny (later the second wife of Anthony Trollope's brother, Thomas Adolphus Trollope). But I fear one cannot agree with Mr. Rolfe that this letter also proves that Dickens "supported" two Ternan girls. There must be hundreds of persons who have financed the study of young singers abroad during the last 150 years without having enjoyed sexual relations with either them or their sisters.

Except for reviews and letters, this was the juncture at which I first entered the picture by publishing in *College English*[21] an article bearing the same title as this volume. This may, therefore, be a good point at which to pause and take a look at the Wright-Storey "evidence" before going on to the later writers who have sought to add to it, especially Ada Nisbet and Felix Aylmer. Meanwhile, however, let it be frankly stated that though J. W. T. Ley, T. W. Hill, Leslie C. Staples, Pansy Pakenham, Mary G. Dickins, Gerald G. Grubb, and a few others have all dealt judiciously with this matter in articles and reviews, so far as the biographers in general are concerned, Wright-Storey has triumphantly carried the day; not even Edgar Johnson[22] gives his reader any inkling that there is a difference of opinion. Felix Aylmer makes the amazing assertion that Wright-Storey "has been repeated by subsequent biographers, though with circumspection, as though the documentation was not entirely adequate." This is an excellent statement

biography. T. W. Hill remarked justly of Lindsay's use of the word "lie" that it is "reminiscent of a vulgar and quarrelsome urchin shouting in a street row."

[20] In *Nineteenth Century Fiction*, Vol. IV (1949), 343–44.

[21] Vol. XI (1950), 373–82.

[22] *Charles Dickens, His Tragedy and Triumph* (Simon and Schuster, 1952). This work was republished in 1965 by Little, Brown.

of what biographers in general have *not* done, the most important exceptions being W. H. Bowen in *Charles Dickens and His Family*[23] and G. G. L. DuCann in *The Love Lives of Charles Dickens*,[24] both of whom lay all the cards on the table and return the only possible verdict "*not proven.*"[25]

[23] Privately printed by W. Heffer & Sons, Ltd., 1956.

[24] (Frederick Muller, 1961).

[25] In their Preface to *The Trollopes, The Chronicle of a Writing Family* (Columbia University Press, 1945), Lucy Poate Stebbins and Richard Poate Stebbins write: "Contemporaneous rumors concerning the private conduct of . . . Ellen Lawless Ternan, although impossible to ignore, had in our judgment no basis in fact." Mrs. Dickins (Sir Herbert Grierson's daughter) contributed a very interesting article, "Dickens Self-Revealed," to *The Dickensian*, Vol. XLII (1945–46), 65–71, 129–33. Insisting that "the proofs [for a liaison between Dickens and Ellen Ternan] are by no means final and beyond dispute," she points out that, on the hypothesis of guilt, "the curious thing about it is that, if Dickens had been a little more of a man of the world, a little more *dishonest*, a little cleverer at conducting an intrigue, the whole thing might have come and gone, and no one would have been much worse for it. But neither he nor Catherine really knew how to deal with this sort of thing. Kate was too stupid and accommodating, and Dickens was too impatient and straight-forward. Between them they made a pretty mess of it; Kate agreed to leave her home and children, and Dickens lost his peace of mind for ever. For Dickens himself did not, and knew that he did not, approve what had happened. Like St. Paul he found himself in a quandary; he was doing and continued to do, something that fundamentally he did not wish to do; or at least that he wished had never happened." See, too, T. W. Hill, "Dickens Biography from Forster to the Present Day," Pt. II, *Dickensian*, Vol. XLVII (1951), 72–79.

Dickens biography reached its nadir in a maundering and meandering book by Michael Harrison, *Charles Dickens: A Sentimental Journey in Search of an Unvarnished Portrait* (Cassell, 1953). "Ellen, *and her Mamma*, were what a later generation came to call 'gold diggers.' " Dickens was jealous of Wilkie Collins's "literary and sexual prowess" and "inspired to emulate his young friend in every way." Having learned about Ellen, "we shall probably learn, in due course, about some other women in Dickens's life." Actually, even now, "it is only their names that we do not know." If his true relations with Ellen

I ask the reader to keep these facts in mind as we proceed to the Wright-Storey "evidence."

IV

First, then, as to Thomas Wright. Canon William Benham (1831–1910), a Church of England cleric, who was a close friend of Ellen Ternan and her husband,

had been known in his own time, it "would have inevitably coloured the reputation of Dickens in a manner not very dissimilar to that in which the reputation of Oscar Wilde was clouded." But Mr. Harrison, who does not object to a contradiction, provided only that both alternatives are slanderous, also argues that it *was* known! Dickens bought Gad's Hill because it gave him a chance to move Kate and the family out of London, thus making it easier for him to carry on with Ellen (there's chronology for you)! But Ellen also "came down to Gad's Hill and stayed there with Dickens's sister-in-law, Georgy, and his children—including his two grown-up daughters." Georgina's motive for tolerating such goings-on was "her jealous hatred" of her sister: "let *anybody* have the love that she had tried for, and had not succeeded in obtaining." Thackeray knew the truth; he "even hinted that the mistress of Dickens's other household—his official household, if we may call it so—was a mistress in the other sense of the word." (This, of course, is exactly what Thackeray denied and angered Dickens by referring to Ellen Ternan in the course of denying.) Queen Victoria knew also, and "while Mrs. Dickens remained alive, to threaten an exposure, there could be no question of an honour for Dickens." It is difficult for Mr. Harrison to avoid smearing anybody whom he has occasion to refer to even marginally; hypothetically he smears Mrs. Dickens herself when, with asinine solemnity, he debates whether Dickens's marriage was what we call a "shotgun wedding" (an idea which has never occurred to anybody except him), as solemnly decides against the notion, and concludes instead that Dickens married Kate because he was in love with her sister Mary. Dickens did not believe in God (on another page he is an agnostic). When he parted from his wife he also parted from his art and became a public entertainer. He was so badly shaken by the Staplehurst railroad accident because he knew that, in surviving it, he had escaped "the meet and just penalty for sin." Why sinners must die in railroad accidents, Mr. Harrison does not explain, except to remind us that Carker was killed by a train in *Dombey and*

15

told Wright—that is to say, Wright informed his readers that
Canon Benham had told him—that Ellen Ternan, having brooded
through the years over her connection with Dickens until the
memory had poisoned her life and she had come to loathe the very
thought of her "intimacy" with the novelist, had finally "dis-
burdened her mind" and confessed her sin to Canon Benham.

As Ethel Barrymore once created a theatrical legend by re-
marking, "That's all there is. There isn't any more."

Charles Dickens is dead. Ellen Ternan is dead. Canon
Benham is dead. As of 1934 it was not possible to interrogate any

---

Son. Actually Dickens met an equally vile form of death: he drank himself into
his grave. He may have had epilepsy; Harrison even misinterprets a statement
of Arthur Waugh's to mean that he may have had a venereal disease.

None of this, however, is very important. What really distresses me is
what has been said by honest, careful, gifted scholars whose work, in all other
aspects, I admire and respect. In his *Charles Dickens: A Critical Introduction*
(Longmans, 1958), K. J. Fielding asserts both that "there is no reasonable doubt"
that Ellen Ternan became Dickens's mistress (p. 161) and that "we still do not
know exactly what their relations were" (p. 192). In what is perhaps the best
all-round critical study of Dickens's art that we have yet acquired, *The Flint and
the Flame: The Artistry of Charles Dickens* (University of Missouri Press, 1963),
Earle Davis carelessly permits himself to write that "the new biographical *fact*
was *established* after a number of years" (italics mine), which is exactly what
did not happen. But the passage which really makes me wish to cry "Shame, J.
Steerforth!" is in Philip Collins's otherwise unexceptionable discussion of
Dickens's charitable work with Angela Burdett-Coutts: "It is one of the ironies
of Dickens's life that his connection with Urania Cottage [which was the name
of the refuge] ceased through his involvement in an affair which might have
qualified yet another girl for entrance into a Home for Fallen Women" (*Dickens
and Crime* [Macmillan, 1962], 111). However innocent Ellen Ternan may
have been of the charges that have been made against her, I must confess that
when I survey the blunders which otherwise almost inerrant writers have made
in discussing her, I am sometimes tempted to wonder whether she may not have
been a witch who continues to befuddle her adversaries from another world!

one of these persons or call them in rebuttal. None could speak in behalf of the accused.

Does it not seem strange that the English-speaking world should have been called upon on such a basis to asperse the memory of a Victorian lady during her children's lifetime and to revise its whole conception of the personal character of one of the greatest novelists who ever lived? And does it not seem even stranger that it should have eagerly embraced the opportunity to do both of these things?

In the *Daily Express* article it was suggested that Ellen Ternan had confided to Canon Benham in his clerical capacity. Thomas Wright was a Plymouth Brother. A Plymouth Brother may be, one would hope, a gentleman, and a gentleman does not betray a secret which a friend (above all, a woman friend) has communicated in confidence. A Plymouth Brother, unfamiliar with auricular confession as practiced in any communion, might nevertheless fail to understand how serious a charge he was making against an Anglican clergyman. For Canon Benham was an Anglo-Catholic, and Ellen Ternan's husband was an ordained deacon in his own church.

After his article had appeared, these considerations were brought to Wright's attention. He was also given to understand that Ellen Ternan herself was decidedly Protestant in her religious feelings, and that she was not the sort of woman who would be likely to "confess" a "sin" to a clergyman. The confessional angle, accordingly, disappeared altogether when the story was repeated in book form.

When J. W. T. Ley asked Wright why he had not sought corroborative evidence for so serious a charge, Wright replied, with incredible naïveté, that it had not occurred to him that any-

body would doubt his word! Having learned in the most unpleasant way possible that there were such unpleasantly suspicious
persons in the world, he proceeded to gather "evidence." Ley once
told me that he had certain knowledge that Wright had failed to
get this material printed in at least one London newspaper and one
English literary weekly. What he finally did was to leave it to be
given to the world posthumously in his *Autobiography*.[26]

This time it is no English cleric whose testimony is presented.
Instead, Wright and his readers have considerably come down in
the world, and we are being regaled with the gossip of a Mrs.
Martha Goldring, "who in her younger days had worked for Mr.
Charles Dickens when he lived *sub rosa* at Linden Grove, Nun-
head, S.E."

But it is still a case of what the soldier said. Mrs. Goldring
told the story to a later employer, Mrs. John Summerson. And
Mrs. Summerson told her daughter. And Mrs. Summerson's
daughter told Mr. Wright.

We have now entered the happy world of Gilbert and Sullivan. But let us proceed boldly.

The gentleman for whom Mrs. Goldring worked was known
as Mr. Tringham, and he was engaged in writing a mystery story.
From another resident of Linden Grove, Wright learned that Mr.
Tringham's house had "special external sliding venetian shutters
at the back," similar to those which Dickens used at Gad's Hill.
This brilliantly alert spirit was also acquainted with a jobmaster
who told him that "he had often driven Dickens and fetched him
from and to Linden Grove." When Wright looked up the rate
books, he found that the occupier of this house during the period
involved was successively listed as Frances Turnham, Thomas

[26] (Herbert Jenkins, 1936).

18

Turnham, Thomas Tringham, and Charles Tringham. The house was vacated in July, 1870, the month after Dickens died.

But there is something else. There is plenty of evidence. That is to say, there is the kind of evidence which satisfies those who cry for a cipher, and who can prove by this means that Bacon (or somebody else) wrote Shakespeare or that the Kaiser (or some other current villain) is referred to in the Book of Daniel or the Revelation. For Dickens's last novels are crammed with Ellen. She is Estella in *Great Expectations*, and she is Bella Wilfer in *Our Mutual Friend*, and she is Helena Landless in *The Mystery of Edwin Drood*. The names prove it. The names and the fact that Dickens never portrayed such girls as these before he knew Ellen. "I love money, and want money—want it dreadfully. I hate to be poor, offensively poor," says Bella. And, according to Wright, "Miss Ternan was grateful to Dickens for the notice he took of her, flattered by his name and wealth, and pleased with the presents he gave her, but she did not love him." Pip (who is Dickens) loves the cold Estella in defiance of all reason and promise, but Estella marries Drummle (who apparently is Dickens also!) because Drummle is a man of means. But Ellen did not marry Dickens, nor anybody else during his lifetime; so something seems to go wrong here. There is trouble too with Lucie Manette of *A Tale of Two Cities*, for she is another kind of girl altogether. But—triumphant confirmation!—Lucie's lover, Charles Darnay, whom she did marry, had the same initials as Charles Dickens! And when he arrives at Helena Landless, Wright regards his case as proved, for Helena Landless is obviously a variant of Ellen Lawless Ternan![27]

[27] Suppose, for that matter, it is. Does the use of a variant version of a person's *name* in fiction imply that the *character* of the original is reproduced?

19

Practically all who accept Wright-Storey follow this Baconian line, generally without giving Wright the dubious credit of having originated it. Felix Aylmer, showing much more consciousness than is at all common to the brethren that Dickens's later heroines are not all of a piece, attempts to show that the changes from one girl to another reflect changing aspects of the still-developing Dickens-Ternan relationship. But the first prize unquestionably goes to Mr. Lindsay, who makes Dr. Manette Dickens, with the Bastille (if I read him aright) the symbol of Dickens's unhappy marriage. But, then, according to Mr. Lindsay, Dickens is also both Carton and Darnay, so that he "gets the satisfaction of nobly giving up the girl and yet mating with her." This is very ingenious, though I think it a weakness in his argument that Mr. Lindsay does not explain what additional satisfaction he derives from also being her father, for I should have thought that the suggestion of incest involved might have attracted a Freudian (I could play this game as well as anybody if I chose to put my mind to it). Mr. Lindsay believes too that "this girl whom he called Nelly [Ellen Ternan] liberated him [Dickens] from the ghost of Little Nell,"

Was Fagin a portrait of the Bob Fagin who was so kind to Dickens in his youth? Are we really supposed to consider Rosa Bud and Helena Landless such unpleasant girls that Dickens could not have created them without first having been disillusioned in Ellen Ternan? What about the noble, heroic, and high-minded Lizzie Hexam, of *Our Mutual Friend*, who is as much a part of this period as Estella, Bella Wilfer, or anybody else? (As far as that is concerned, Bella's cupidity is the least convincing aspect of her characterization, clearly determined by the more sensational aspects of the plot, and not by something that was oppressing the writer's own mind.) And why is Fanny Dorrit ignored? Can it be that it is because, though she is both mercenary and pert, Dickens created her *before*, according to scandalmongers' chronology, he fell in love with Ellen Ternan? How would Mrs. Dickens fare if all the shrewish matrons in Dickens's novels were to be taken as a composite portrait of her?

20

and I do not doubt that the later heroines are more realistically convincing than the earlier ones. But then, so are the later heroes. Will someone please be kind enough to explain what young *man* among Dickens's friends was responsible for that? Or could it be simply that Dickens was growing as an artist clear up to his death?

V

But what, now, of Mrs. Perugini's evidence? Must not the testimony of Dickens's own daughter be considered conclusive? Hardly, in the form in which we have it. For the essential point about Mrs. Perugini's testimony is that we do not have Mrs. Perugini's testimony. Every statement Mrs. Perugini made about her father during her lifetime was highly laudatory. Concerning what she told Miss Storey we have only Miss Storey's report, published ten years after Mrs. Perugini's death.[28]

[28] It is true that in a letter to the London *Times Literary Supplement*, July 29, 1939 (p. 453), Bernard Shaw came to Miss Storey's rescue by declaring that Mrs. Perugini had on two different occasions told him what she told Miss Storey, once toward the end of the nineteenth century and again shortly before her own death. Miss Nisbet (*Dickens and Ellen Ternan*, 85–86) chides me for ignoring this statement and citing only what Shaw wrote in his introduction to the edition of *Great Expectations* published by the Limited Editions Club in 1937: "Dickens, when he let himself go in Great Expectations, was separated from his wife and free to make more intimate acquaintance with women than a domesticated man can. I know nothing of his adventures in this phase of his career, though I daresay a good deal of it will be dug out by the little sect of anti-Dickensites whose fanaticism has been provoked by the Dickens Fellowships, and threatens to become as pathological as Bacon-Shakespear. It is not necessary to suggest a love affair; for Dickens could get from a passing glance a hint which he could expand into a full-grown character." Her rebuke is just to the extent that I had not seen the *TLS* statement at the time I wrote my *College English* article, though I did find it before Miss Nisbet's book appeared and referred to it in my *Introduction to Dickens* (Scott, Foresman, 1952), p. 425, n. 4. But the fact that Shaw made the *TLS* statement does not cancel out the other one; it

I am *not* saying that we must choose between accepting Miss Storey's statement at face value and maintaining that Mrs. Perugini and/or Miss Storey deliberately lied about Dickens. There are other possibilities.

Mrs. Perugini, who was nineteen at the time her father and mother separated, may have been mistaken about her father's relations with Ellen Ternan. Or she may, in her old age (as Mark Twain once said of himself), have remembered only the things that never happened. I do not know whether such a suggestion could cover the case or not. I say frankly that I very much wish it might, for I greatly dislike believing that all the statements Mrs. Perugini gave to the world about Dickens during her lifetime were deliberately insincere and that she wished to go on record at last as spitting on her father's grave.

Again, Miss Storey may have misunderstood Mrs. Perugini in such a manner as, after Mrs. Perugini's death in 1929, *to have permitted herself to interpret what Mrs. Perugini had told her in*

simply illustrates his not unfamiliar habit of speaking on both sides of the question. In 1935 Walter Dexter attacked Shaw ("Mr. Shaw Taken to Task," *Dickensian*, Vol. XXXI [1935], 295) for having stated ("A Letter from Bernard Shaw," *Time and Tide*, Vol. XVI [1935], 1111–12) that in 1899 he had persuaded Mrs. Perugini not to burn her father's letters to his wife, she not desiring to have them "exposed . . . to the pryings of the Dickens Fellowships and Dickens fans generally whom she abhorred." Since the Dickens Fellowship was not founded until 1902, this statement does not give Shaw high rank as a historian. Fourteen years later, in a message to *The Dickensian* for their *David Copperfield* centenary number (Vol. XLV [1949], 118), characteristically crying down *David Copperfield* in favor of *Great Expectations*, Shaw speaks of "a quite new and unDickensish Estella, *not yet identified, whom he* [Dickens] *must have met after his separation from his wife*" (italics mine). An Estella not yet identified whom Dickens met after his separation from his wife could not, of course, be Ellen Ternan. I think, Miss Nisbet, we had better both give up Bernard Shaw; he is not going to be of much use to either of us.

the light of the scandal which had meanwhile been set off by Thomas Wright. Miss Storey writes extraordinarily badly, and there is nothing in her book which would incline one to trust her judgment in the evaluation of evidence. She is vague about her authorities; she does not quote accurately from sources which can be checked, not even Dickens's novels;[29] and scholars who have attempted to question her tell me that she has either refused to see them or shown herself extremely disinclined to answer specific questions. Her vanity and her naïveté in literary matters may be gauged from the fact that she prints in *Dickens and Daughter* not only a portrait of herself but also one of her mother! That Mrs. Perugini told Miss Storey something I make no question. But it need not necessarily have been just what Miss Storey recorded.[30] If we disregard Bernard Shaw's contradictory testimony,[31] Miss Storey (girl as she was then) was the only person whom Mrs. Perugini ever made her confidante in this delicate matter. Why? Even if we rule out the members of her own family on the hypothetical ground that they knew the truth as well as she did but

[29] For that matter, Dame Una Pope-Hennessy does not accurately quote Miss Storey!

[30] Be it remarked parenthetically that Ellen Ternan may also have told Canon Benham "something." But this would not prove that she told him exactly what Thomas Wright remembered and/or recorded. There is no doubt that Mrs. Dickens was jealous of Ellen Ternan; as an older woman, looking back over her life, Ellen might well have regretted this, and she need not have been Dickens's mistress either then or later to reproach herself with having thus thoughtlessly contributed to the final collapse of the Dickens marriage. This kind of thing, too, Canon Benham *might* have felt that he was at liberty to communicate to Thomas Wright (though, as it turned out, he could not have been more wrong), whereas, unless he was a faithless cleric and no gentleman besides, he would not be at liberty to pass on a confession of a serious infraction of the accepted moral code.

[31] See note 28 above.

wished to suppress it, there still remains the fact that she was upon terms of cordiality with a great many persons who knew far more about Dickens than Gladys Storey will ever learn. Why did she not confide in them? On any hypothesis, the answers to such questions are difficult.

To be sure, Mrs. Perugini herself was a complicated character. She claimed, on doubtful grounds, that she married Charles Collins without loving him, to get away from her father. She is also recorded as having said of herself: "I wish I had never been born. I am glad now that my little boy did not live, for he would probably have inherited all my faults." Why was her tenderness for her mother apparently so late in awakening? If it was Dickens who kept her from inviting her mother to her first wedding, why did she not herself invite her to the second, four years after Dickens's death? Do not these facts and others like them suggest that Dickens may have been telling the truth when he said that his wife and children had little or nothing to do with each other? And may not Kate's later attitude toward her mother and father have been determined by the remorse which followed upon afterthought and reconsideration rather than by anything she felt at the time of the break? Was there even an element of self-castigation in her reported remark to Miss Storey that her father was "a very wicked man"?[32]

VI

We must now consider the fresh evidence introduced by Professor Nisbet[33] and by Mr. Aylmer.[34] I cannot claim to be the "onlie begetter" of Miss Nisbet's book, but I had an important

[32] See, further, Gerald G. Grubb's review of *Dickens and Ellen Ternan*, *Dickensian*, Vol. XLIX (1952), p. 125, n. 1.

share in it,[35] and to be blunt I must say that there are literary offspring I could have owned with more pride. Mr. Aylmer, too, has me considerably on his mind; indeed I am something of a King Charles's head to Mr. Aylmer; at one point he even wonders out loud whether he will not shock me. Dear Mr. Aylmer, I have been shocked by experts.

Before I come to Miss Nisbet, however, I must note one earlier and less consequential reply to my *College English* article,

[33] Ada Nisbet, *Dickens & Ellen Ternan* (University of California Press, 1952).

[34] Felix Aylmer, *Dickens Incognito* (Rupert Hart-Davis, 1959).

[35] "These notes would probably have remained unpublished, except as they might have found a place in the larger study now in progress, if it had not been for the violence of certain recent attacks upon the reliability and integrity of those critics and scholars who have accepted the story of Dickens's liaison with Ellen Ternan as fact. . . . I respect the critics and writers under fire, who include such people as Dame Una Pope-Hennessy, Hesketh Pearson, Edmund Wilson, Lionel Stevenson, Clifton Fadiman, and W. Somerset Maugham among others [does Miss Nisbet regard all these persons as critics and scholars?], and I resent the nature and tone of the attacks. This volume is the result." "Nor do Dickensians like Mr. Edward Wagenknecht gain anything when they greet each unwelcome discovery as a slander or brand the scholars and biographers who make these discoveries 'peeping Toms,' 'ghouls,' and 'scandalmongers' " (*Dickens and Ellen Ternan*, xiii–xiv, 4–5). I cannot help wondering what a "Dickensian" is, and in what sense I am a "Dickensian." I believe that Dickens was a great writer. So, I suppose, does Miss Nisbet; otherwise I cannot imagine why she wastes so much on time on him, though I must, in all fairness, add that she seems to me never to miss an opportunity to interpret a fact or circumstance to his discredit. Primarily, however, I am an American literature man. I have written a book about Dickens, but I have also written books about Mark Twain, Hawthorne, Irving, etc., etc. Am I, therefore, also a "Twainian," "Hawthornian," "Irvingite," etc., and am I supposed to have a vested interest in everybody I have ever written about? Perhaps the fact that I have written about Marilyn Monroe makes me a "Monrovian." Possibly I should try to cultivate a new respect for myself as a many-sided creature, but I cannot help feeling that all these distinctions have been too lightly won.

that of Professor Richard B. Hudson.[36] This is not, in itself, of any great consequence at this date, but it does illustrate the confusion in which most of the people who have tried to write on this subject have managed to get themselves involved, and in any case it is a part of the history of the controversy and cannot therefore be left out.

Just why Mr. Hudson felt called upon to write this article I have never quite understood. He had previously noticed my article in his "Victorian Bibliography" for 1950, published in *Modern Philology*,[37] where he said:

> This article is an excellent analysis of the alleged evidence presented by Wright and Storey. . . . Mr. Wagenknecht is quite right in asserting that no one has *proved* that such a relationship did exist between Dickens and Ellen Ternan. . . . His conclusions are temperate and judicious.

For this notice I thanked Mr. Hudson by writing him a letter in which some of the problems involved were further discussed, and to which he did not reply.

It is true that, even in *Modern Philology*, Mr. Hudson did not like the "tone" of my article.

> One cannot escape a strong feeling that Mr. Wagenknecht is not wholly dispassionate in his efforts to preserve Dickens's reputation. His heavy irony and his use of such words as "contemptible" and "shameful" do not add much to the argument, especially when his opponents are such unscholarly people as Mr. Wright and Miss Storey.

[36] "The Dickens Affair Again," *College English*, Vol. XIII (1951), 111–13.
[37] Vol. XLVIII (1951), 247.

(Does Mr. Hudson believe that only scholarly people can be shameful and contemptible?)

In his article in *College English* he returns to the attack, but meanwhile I have suffered a sea change, being no longer either "temperate" or "judicious."

He now wishes to be informed "what it is at this distance to 'asperse the memory of a Victorian gentlewoman during her children's lifetime'? Who would have remembered her anyway?" My first thought was to reply, "Her children," which I thought I had made clear. But if you reject the basic principle of Anglo-Saxon justice—that every man is innocent until he is proved guilty—and along with it another principle which I think all persons of fine feeling do accept—that one does not bring unproved or unprovable assertions of evil conduct against the helpless dead—then I suppose, Mr. Hudson, it really makes no difference at all. My critic also informs his readers that he does not "feel so strongly" about Dickens's private character as I seem to feel, and that he is "content to take Dickens as [he] find[s] him."

Concerning Mr. Hudson's feelings on this matter I fear I am no more deeply interested than Mr. Skimpin was in the impressions on Mr. Winkle's mind. But the new material that Mr. Hudson introduces into his discussion at this point cannot be allowed to pass unchallenged. For he is unqualifiedly and demonstrably wrong on every conceivable point.[38]

I had, for example, quoted, as to Dickens's character, from the testimony of those who knew him best, including Tom Trollope, who was, if we follow Wright-Storey, the brother-in-law of the girl Dickens seduced: "Dickens hated a mean action or a mean

---

[38] For my comments on Mr. Hudson from this point on, I am heavily indebted to the late Gerald G. Grubb.

sentiment as one hates something that is physically loathsome to the sight or touch." I had also quoted from Marcus Stone: "Charles Dickens was the best man I have ever known. He was so good that you put his greatness into second place when you knew him." Mr. Hudson asks:

> Now, are these men passing final judgment on the man who in-serted the "Address" in *Household Words?* The man who wrote the so-called "Violated Letter" with its appended retraction? The man who gratuitously insulted his wife in his last will and testa-ment? Professor Wagenknecht should be told that these, to our modern tastes, are mean actions within the limits of Tom Trol-lope's statement.

I am far from believing that Dickens was blameless in this matter, nor do I feel called upon to justify everything he did. But the *Household Words* statement was submitted to Mrs. Dickens for her approval before publication, and the "violated letter," though its writing may have been an act of bad judgment, was not published by him. To be sure, Miss Nisbet thinks he was a liar about this too, but she has not proved it, any more than she has proved the statement she cavalierly throws out that Dickens ar-ranged for the lodgings of Maria and Ellen Ternan in Oxford Street as early as 1858.

As for Dickens's having "insulted" his wife in his will, here is the relevant statement:

> AND I BEQUEATH unto my said son Charles and my son Henry Fielding Dickens, the sum of £8,000 upon trust to invest the same, and from time to time vary the investments thereof, and to pay the annual income thereof to my wife during her life. . . . AND I DESIRE here simply to record the fact that my wife, since

28

our separation by consent, has been in the receipt from me of an annual income of £600, while all the great charges of a numerous and expensive family have devolved wholly upon myself.

There *is* a touch of self-righteousness here, but where is the insult? The statement made was the undisputed truth, and it was not couched in offensive language. Mrs. Dickens's yearly income of £600, during her husband's lifetime, free of all family expenses, was greater than the yearly salary of Dickens's subeditor, W. H. Wills. Her own attorneys felt that Dickens was placing her allowance higher than necessary for a woman on her social level.

Finally, we come to Mr. Hudson's most amazing blunder, which occurs when he quotes approvingly from the *Letters and Memoirs* of Sir William Hardman, editor of the *Morning Post*, concerning the farewell banquet given for Dickens in London, November 2, 1867, before his departure for America:

> But I must say that we, and those who are behind the scenes, did not think much of the list of guests. We were amused to see next day a paragraph stating that his eldest son Charley Dickens's name had been omitted from the list by oversight. Their anxiety to add this, the most respectable of the lot, was amusing. I thought it would have been a good joke if someone had written setting forth the names of those who did *not* accompany him and shed the halo of their respectability over his departure, commencing with Dickens's much-injured wife, whose name was conspicuous by its absence.

Now, what were the facts of this dinner? It is easy to find them, for the *Times*, November 4, devoted two and one-third columns to the affair. Plates were laid for between three hundred and four hundred guests; the galleries were filled with ladies; of

29

the disreputable persons who sat down, more than fifty are now listed in *Webster's Biographical Dictionary*. Bulwer-Lytton presided. Thirteen noblemen were present, thirteen members of the Royal Academy of Arts, eight eminent scientists, four Members of Parliament, and many authors, editors, journalists, and scholars. The speakers were Sir Charles Russell; Captain Houston Stewart, R.N.; Tom Taylor; Sir Charles W. Dilke; J. B. Buckstone; Benjamin Webster; Sir A. H. Layard; Sir Francis Grant; Anthony Trollope; Sir Edwin Landseer; the Lord-Mayor of London; the Chaplain-General of the Armed Forces; and the Lord Chief-Justice of England.

In calling attention to the importance of the Farewell Dinner, the editor of *Harper's Magazine* remarks (June, 1868):

> That there should be no misapprehension upon our part as to the opinion which his [Dickens's] own country holds of him, his departure was signalized by the most flattering ovation which any purely literary man ever received in England. His chief living rival, Sir Edward Bulwer Lytton, an author who was famous before Dickens was ever heard of, and whose fame that of Dickens had eclipsed, was the generous president of the occasion. The Lord Chief Justice of England was a guest. The President of the Royal Academy was another. The guild of Letters and Art united to honor its most illustrious ornament, and the spectacle must have been remarkable and inspiring. There were a great many good things said; and the speech [of the guest] was especially felicitous and generous. And so with the hearty farewell of his friends and brethren, our old friend and critic sailed again for our shores.

Could Sir William Hardman possibly have believed that that was not a respectable dinner? Could he possibly have believed that Mrs. Dickens ought to have been invited? And if he did, does

Mr. Hudson really agree with him? Mrs. Dickens had been separated from her husband for nine years. To invite her would have been an unforgivable insult, and only a madwoman could have accepted such an invitation. As a matter of fact, Mrs. Dickens understood the situation perfectly, and Mark Lemon, who had represented her in the separation proceedings, did attend. She herself wrote Dickens a note, expressing her goodwill, to which he responded.

Dickens was always very careful, after the separation, to avoid wounding his wife in any way. It was her own lawyers who set a restriction in the separation agreement, denying her the right to see her children at Dickens's residence, Tavistock House. Dickens struck it out, saying, "The exception seemed to me to convey an unnecessary slight upon her, and I said she shall see them there or anywhere." When the "violated letter" appeared in print, Dickens hastened to inform his wife that he was not a "consenting party to this publication," that it had "shocked and distressed [him] very much." When he escaped injury in the Staplehurst wreck, Mrs. Dickens, on her part, wrote him a letter of congratulation, to which he replied, thanking her for her good wishes.

Let us, by all means, take Dickens as we find him. But let him be the Dickens of known fact and not of our own or irresponsible persons' imaginations.

VII

Miss Nisbet wrote *Dickens and Ellen Ternan* with a laudable purpose in mind. She wished to settle a literary and biographical controversy by which she professed to be much distressed. I do not believe that she did this, but I do think it a great step forward that she should have been brought to admit that there *is* a controversy.

Up to the time her book appeared, all who believe as she does had simply assumed that there was nothing to argue about. Catherine Hogarth was Dickens's wife, and Ellen Ternan was his mistress, and that was that.

I cannot quite agree with the late Gerald Grubb that, her new material being so scanty as it was, Miss Nisbet ought to have written an article, not a book. It seems to me that though there is nothing new in her earlier chapters, it *is* useful to have all the material brought together and summarized in a temperate and intelligent manner. Grubb accused her of suppressing evidence which did not support her theory. It is true that she omits some points which would militate against her, but it is not necessary to assume that this was maliciously done. Though I disagree with her on almost every page, I frequently admire her fairness and moderation. She frankly gives up on the attempt to establish that Ellen Ternan bore a child, for example, though she must know that this admission considerably weakens her hypothesis. Edmund Wilson does the same in his foreword: "The statement made by Wright that Dickens had children or a child by Ellen is not supported by independent evidence."

Miss Nisbet's new material consists of canceled passages referring to Ellen from Dickens's letters in the Huntington Library and from a pocket diary in the Berg Collection at the New York Public Library,[39] allegedly referring to a code to be used to inform Ellen whether or not to join him on his American reading tour of 1867–68. These have now been deciphered by means of infrared photography.

[39] This had already been discussed by John D. Gordan, in "The Secret of Dickens' Memoranda," in *Bookmen's Holiday: Notes and Studies Written and Gathered in Tribute to Harry Miller Lydenberg* (The New York Public Library, 1943).

There is no possibility of rejecting the evidence of the letters. And I think this evidence clearly establishes the fact that, in some sense of the term, Dickens "loved" Ellen Ternan—"my Darling" and "my dear girl." It does *not*, however, prove that they had sexual relations. If every man is to be considered as having gone to bed with every girl whom at one time or another he has called his darling, one cannot help wondering how much of the world will be left on its feet.

On the other point, however, Miss Nisbet seems to me less fortunate. The code in the diary may well mean exactly what she supposed it to mean, though Grubb argued[40] that its full meaning has not yet been apprehended and that other interpretations are possible. And since, if Ellen had come to America, she would certainly have been chaperoned by her mother, as she seems to have been at Staplehurst and elsewhere,[41] the matter is of very little interest anyway. Dickens was not Maxim Gorky, and he cannot at any point have been so simple as to consider the possibility of touring the United States with a young mistress in tow. Neither, I think, can he have contemplated transporting her in a trunk, as Archbishop Cranmer was supposed to have done with his German wife.

But I must not leave either of these points without pointing out that my feeling that Miss Nisbet has not really proved very much is not peculiar to me or to those who are like-minded with me. On the contrary, it has been freely and fully expressed by those who admire her work most.

First, Edmund Wilson, who, as noted, contributed a fore-

[40] See the review of *Dickens and Ellen Ternan*, as previously cited, and cf. Aylmer's dissenting view, *Dickensian*, Vol. LI (1954), 85–86.
[41] See Bowen, *Charles Dickens and his Family*, 120–21, 132.

word to Miss Nisbet's book: "if Dickens's relations with Ellen Ternan were, as the Dickensians insist, Platonic, he was an even odder case than one had thought."[42]

I submit that if an "if" can be entered, then it is idle to talk of Miss Nisbet as having *proved* her case.

Second, Professor Richard D. Altick, who reviewed Miss Nisbet's book very favorably in the New York *Herald-Tribune Book Review*.[43] In one short notice, Mr. Altick managed to assert twice that Miss Nisbet had established her thesis and once that she hadn't; Ellen might, still, have been just a very good friend of Dickens! Well, I know ambivalence has its values in art, but it does seem to me of doubtful utility in book reviewing. Of course I am not so foolish as to hold Miss Nisbet responsible for Mr. Altick's carelessness, but his review still helps to establish my point that not even her special admirers can consistently argue that she has established her thesis.

My own basic disagreement with her, however, is yet to be stated. In the first place, she shows not the slightest comprehension of what my article was all about. It was never my purpose to prove that Ellen Ternan was *not* Dickens's mistress. This does not require proving from me or anybody else. The burden of proof rests on the other side. What I said was that *nobody had proved she was* and that therefore nobody had a right to state the connection as an established fact. And on this point I have been unwillingly supported, as I have now demonstrated, by Edmund Wilson, Richard

[42] Odder than who had thought? and upon what assumption? If the "one" indicates Mr. Wilson and those who take his view, then the previous assumption would seem to have been that, after his separation from his wife, Dickens made Ellen Ternan his mistress. A wide variety of moral judgments might well be passed upon such an act. But what on earth is "odd" about it?

[43] December 21, 1952, p. 5.

B. Hudson, and Richard D. Altick. My article was not primarily a *defense* of Dickens and Ellen Ternan. It was primarily an *attack* upon sloppiness and irresponsibility in critical and biographical writing.

Furthermore, even if, in her 1952 book, Miss Nisbet had completely succeeded in doing what she set out to do—that is, to prove that Ellen Ternan was the mistress of Charles Dickens and thus close the case forever[44]—this could not possibly affect anything that I wrote about her predecessors in the year 1950. They did not, any of them, in 1950 or in any previous year, possess the facts which Miss Nisbet made known in 1952. Either her evidence was wholly trifling (and her book therefore an impertinent superfluity) or else her predecessors accused Dickens on insufficient evidence or no evidence whatever. Consequently I found it impossible to relish Miss Nisbet as a gallant Britomart, riding to the rescue

[44] "Mr. T. W. Hill, an ardent Dickensian [all "Dickensians" are "ardent" as all actors are "sterling"], has remarked that 'all that is required is reasonable substantiation of statements. Give us substantiation and the facts must be accepted at once.' Here, then, is that substantiation—in the incontrovertible hand of Dickens himself" (*Dickens and Ellen Ternan*, 7). I hope it is not necessary to say that the writer of this book does not pledge himself never to change his mind about anything, should evidence which really substantiates points at present unsubstantiated be presented. Scandalmongers may guess right as well as wrong, and even a good case may be so badly bungled in its presentation as to be reduced to nonsense. The point about Ellen Ternan's presence in Dickens's company at the Staplehurst accident was thus quite innocently bungled by dear old Mrs. Thomas Whiffen, than whom nobody could have been less inclined to scandalmongering, in her autobiography of her years on the stage, *Keeping Off the Shelf* (Dutton, 1928), and she was blasted by Sir Henry Fielding Dickens and others, yet Ellen's presence at Staplehurst would now seem to have been established. Some of Dickens's biographers not only know what happened but at every point know also just how Dickens and Ellen Ternan felt about what was happening, but I have never claimed mediumistic powers; I can only deal with the evidence that has been made available up to this point—and leave the future unbound.

35

of all the noble writers whom I had so wickedly maligned. As far as they knew, they were talking through their hats. Whether Miss Nisbet was right or wrong in 1952, they were still talking through their hats. As of 1950 they were exactly what I called them. They were scandalmongers.

VIII

Mr. Aylmer, I fear, finds me an even tougher morsel to swallow than Miss Nisbet does; I hope, therefore, that he will not think me offensive when I say that I like his tone a good deal better than hers. Indeed I find Mr. Aylmer offensive only when he talks about "professors." Whether he applies it to me or to Gerald Grubb, Mr. Aylmer apparently finds "professor" a dirty word. It would be quite as reasonable, I think, if I were to use "actor" in a pejorative sense. Indeed, it would be more so, for when I write about literature and biography, I am functioning in my own field, and when Mr. Aylmer does these things, he is not. I shall not do it, however, partly because I do not honestly believe professors to be superior to actors and partly because I cannot think that Mr. Aylmer deserves such a slur. His ability as a research man seems to me, generally speaking, quite equal to that of most professors, and when he becomes absurd, I could match him, absurdity for absurdity, without referring to anybody outside my own field.[45]

[45] Occasionally Mr. Aylmer misunderstands me. On p. 49 (*Dickens Incognito*) he finds "incomplete" a search which I never even suggested that I had made, and on p. 59 he seems to confuse me with J. W. T. Ley. But I cannot claim to have anything to do with his wildest speculations. On p. 60 he has Dickens presumably consulting George Henry Lewes as a specialist on the extralegal ménage; on p. 63 he speculates as to whether Ellen had been "threatened" with twins; on p. 64 he even suggests that Dickens may have kept Holy Week

In the present instance, Mr. Aylmer's researches have been centered upon that same pocket diary in the Berg Collection which had already interested Dr. Gordan and Miss Nisbet. The diary contains a number of references to "Sl" and shows Dickens often going to "Sl." What the American scholars had passed over was made meaningful to Mr. Aylmer by his knowledge of English geography. He would seem to have established that Ellen and "M" (who could have been her mother but was more likely her sister Maria) lived at Slough from 1867 to 1870 and that Dickens frequently stayed there. So far, so good, and a creditable piece of research, and of course a strengthening of the argument for those who believe as Mr. Aylmer does.

If Mr. Aylmer had stopped here, there would be nothing to do except congratulate him—and thank him for an interesting addition to Dickensian knowledge. Unfortunately, however, his imagination was intrigued by the word "Arrival" in the diary under the date of April 13, 1867. Mr. Aylmer did not know what had arrived, but he hoped it might have been a baby. No registration of such a birth was found at Somerset House, but Mr. Aylmer found that on May 20, 1867, registration was made in the District of Lambeth, of the birth of a son, Francis Charles Tringham, to Francis Thomas Tringham, "House Painter Journeyman," and his wife, Elizabeth Tringham, formerly Stanley. Having searched the records at York Road Hospital, where Francis Charles Tringham was said to have been born on May 10, Mr. Aylmer found no record of such a birth; he concluded, therefore, that

(of all the weeks in the year) free of reading engagements because a baby was expected! In his Postscript, indeed, he is so puffed up over his short-lived exaltation over having found one baby that he promptly begins to look round for another one!

37

Francis Charles Tringham was the son of Ellen Ternan by Charles Dickens, and that the birth certificate had been falsified to give him a pair of legitimate parents.

An accomplished comedian in the theater, Mr. Aylmer now proved himself a master of unconscious humor on the printed page by detecting in the registration certificate itself "hints of Dickens in every detail." (No "professor" could have done better.)

> Francis was the masculine form of the name borne by both Mrs. Ternan and her eldest daughter. Charles was his own. The declared father's name reproduced the two Christian names under which he appeared at different dates in the Peckham rate-books. The mother's name Elizabeth had the same initial as Ellen's, and only the initial was included in the signature.

And so on and so on; it would be cruel to quote it all. But it adds up to a perfect parody of what all the advocates of "close reading" who are training their poor, helpless students on James Joyce & Co. are turning out.

> It was possible, even, to see Charles choosing his profession. He had recently been hanging pictures at Gad's Hill. Probably he had done some housepainting as well. As for journeyman, the travelling involved in his reading tours surely justified that description. In short, if Charles had gone to the length of composing a fictitious birth-certificate, it could hardly be more closely packed with internal evidence of his handiwork than this.

Evidently Dickens was trying to work in as many references to himself as possible. Having concealed his indiscretion from everybody else, he was leaving clues for Mr. Aylmer (whose coming he must have foreseen, and for whom he evidently had a fellow feeling) to unravel in the year 1959. Charles Dickens was not a novelist. He was a professional concocter of the old-fashioned kind of picture-puzzle on which some of us were brought up: "How many hidden faces can you find in this picture?"

We shall never know what mischievous gremlin tampered with the York Road Hospital records (or with Mr. Aylmer's eyes) the day he inspected them. But when Graham Storey followed him to check on his report, lo and behold, all the material was there: Francis Charles Tringham was the legitimate son of the house-painter Francis Thomas Tringham and his wife Elizabeth, and he was born on May 10, just as the registration certificate said he was. Mr. Storey published a photostat copy of the record in the *Sunday Times*, December 13, 1959, and commented:

> Mr. Aylmer's chief evidence for the elaborate plan of deception supposedly practised by Dickens therefore collapses. There is in fact no connection between Dickens and the house-painter and his wife, nor any evidence that the entry "Arrival" in the diary for April 13th, 1867, which set Mr. Aylmer off on his search, has any reference whatever to the birth of a child.

Mr. Aylmer met the issue head-on. In his own words, his error called for "a very substantial apology" and "as wide publicity for the correction as I can secure." But *Dickens Incognito* was not suppressed, and when he published *The Drood Case*,[46] he cited it as one of his authorities, insisting that his "gross mis-statement of fact" on this one point did not mean that, in other connections, "such a reference must be valueless, and the least said about the matter the better."

It must be admitted, I think, that if those who believe in the Dickens-Ternan liaison are correct, they have been dogged by

[46] (Rupert Hart-Davis, 1964).

39

singular ill fortune, not to say ineptitude, all along the line. Both Wright and Miss Storey presented their views under conditions admitting of no check by any other person (as Mr. DuCann remarks, Wright "always calls his alleged informants from the tomb to the witness-box"), and while both Miss Nisbet and Mr. Aylmer made genuine contributions, she entertained larger claims for herself than her work substantiates, while he perpetrated one of the most embarrassing blunders in recent literary scholarship.

IX

Where, then, are we left? I think we are left in the very uncomfortable position of being compelled to admit that we do not know everything. In some sense of the word, we may be sure that Charles Dickens loved Ellen Ternan. Various circumstances seem to suggest that the relationship between them did not permanently remain wholly Platonic. I will even grant that there are enough of these so that the accumulation justifies more suspicion than could properly be based on any or all of them taken singly. Beyond that we cannot honestly go.

It must at once be added, however, that some of these circumstances would justify greater suspicion if we were dealing with a different sort of man. There seems no reason to doubt that Dickens was very generous toward the whole Ternan family. With many men, perhaps with most men, we could be sure that some payment was exacted for this. But Dickens was a great giver, and he took on a good many persons from whom he neither received nor expected any return. For this same reason, one is a little surprised, if the story be correctly reported, by Mrs. Dickens's indignation when the piece of jewelry intended for Ellen at the time of *The Frozen Deep* was delivered to her by mistake. Here, again, with many husbands, this would have constituted clear evidence of infidelity or infatuation. But it was an accepted thing for Dickens to make gifts to those who acted with him, men and women both, and he cannot possibly have been infatuated with all of them. If Mrs. Dickens did not know this, then she must have been even less familiar with his affairs than we have hitherto assumed.

May I repeat that my article is primarily not a defense but an attack and that something larger than either Charles Dickens or Ellen Ternan is at stake, that something being the integrity of scholarship itself. I have no quarrel with anybody who states that, in his judgment, the facts which have been established concerning the relationship between Charles Dickens and Ellen Ternan indicate that they were lovers, but I do quarrel with those who state this conclusion as an established fact, for it is not an established fact. What I am asking for is a distinction between fact and theory, between fact and assumption. When assumptions are made, I want them labeled assumption, and any scholar who is not willing to grant me this is engaged in a business for which he has no gift.

Since Miss Nisbet has set me the example of resenting, let me try my hand at resentment too. I resent the tone, the attitude, and the point of view that has been manifested in the discussion of the Dickens-Ternan problem all along the line. I resent it if Dickens and Ellen Ternan were innocent, and I still resent it if they were (if that is the word to use) guilty. I resent it in most of the biographers who have concerned themselves directly with the matter,[47] and I resent it even more in those who have made casual

[47] Not all the biographers. Not Edgar Johnson, for example. As I have said, I think him at fault for his failure to indicate the shaky nature of the evidence upon which the assumption he accepts depends, but there is no trace of anything scornful or holier-than-thou in his attitude. Mr. Aylmer, too, deserves credit for his sympathetic attitude toward Ellen Ternan. Though he believes her

reference to it, generally without quite knowing what they were talking about. Only the other day I saw a reference to the disparity between Victorian moral professions and Victorian conduct, in which the scandalous private lives of Dickens, Thackeray, and George Eliot were casually referred to! What circumstance in Thackeray's life the writer had in mind (if he has a mind), I do not know. The morally earnest George Eliot was the faithful common-law wife of George Henry Lewes under circumstances which abundantly justified her course to her own conscience. One may agree with her or disagree with her, but anyone who considers her an abandoned woman is a fool. And if the worst that any responsible person now believes about Dickens could be firmly established (as distinguished from what was, at the outset, recklessly implied, and what many uninformed persons think they believe), what he did was to marry a woman with whom he was hopelessly mismated and with whom he grew steadily more unhappy through the years (as she with him), and after their separation, under circumstances which pretty well ruled out the possibility of divorce, he formed an alliance with another woman whom he devotedly loved and whom he continued to love until he died. What are all these people? Coptic monks? What kind of standards do they adhere to? Are they all ascetic saints in their private lives? It may be so, but I have known no gloating saints. John Greenleaf Whittier came as close to being a saint as any man I have studied closely, and this is what Whittier wrote when Henry Ward Beecher was accused as an adulterer: "I love Beecher and believe in him. He has done good to thousands. If he has fallen into temp-

---

to have been Dickens's mistress, he has done more than any other writer in his camp to correct the wholly unwarranted picture of her as a scheming, cold-hearted, unprincipled little minx which some of his predecessors had drawn.

tation I shall feel grieved, but would be ashamed of myself were I less his friend."

Let it be noted that upon no hypothesis can Ellen Ternan have been the *cause* of the separation between Dickens and his wife. At the very most she can only have been the occasion. They would surely have separated sooner or later even if Dickens had never seen her; indeed the great tragedy is not that they separated but that they ever married, or that having married, they did not separate long before they did. The authenticity of the so-called Stark-Thomson letter has been much disputed, but since it was written for propaganda purposes, it may well be authentic without being wholly truthful, and if we accept it at face value, then we must also believe that it was the Hogarths who took the initiative in moving for a separation and that Dickens did his utmost to avoid an open break.[48] However Dickens may have *felt* about Ellen Ternan in 1858, no reasonable person now believes that he committed adultery at that time. Aylmer conjectured that physical relations were not established before 1864 or 1865, and Gerald Grubb, unwilling to commit himself to the existence of a genuine liaison at any date, also felt that it could not have begun earlier than this. Why the long delay? Ellen could not have been holding out for marriage, for she never had it, and she must always have known that it was impossible. All the evidence shows that Dickens was generous to the Ternans from the beginning, and she could not

[48] It also puts Kate, along with Mamie, in her father's camp. Bernard Shaw wrote (*Time and Tide*, Vol. XVI [1935], 1111–12) that "the initiative in the separation came from the wife, and was long resisted by the husband." See K. J. Fielding, "Charles Dickens and His Wife—Fact or Fantasy," *Études Anglaises*, Vol. VIII (1955), 212–22; William J. Carlton, "Mr. and Mrs. Dickens: The Thomson-Stark Letter," *Notes and Queries*, N.S. Vol. VII (1960), 145–47. Cf. Johnson, *Charles Dickens, His Tragedy and Triumph*, 918–20.

possibly have believed that her giving him what he wanted would make him less generous. If she held him off for six or seven years, or even for four or five, is it not much more likely that she had conscientious scruples to overcome and that she did not achieve this lightly if indeed she achieved it at all? And, for that matter, Ellen being as young as she was, why should we doubt that Dickens had the same battle to wage with himself?

I am not saying that this is what happened. I do not know what happened. What I *am* saying is that even if it did happen, there is nobody in this drama—not Dickens, not Catherine, not Ellen Ternan—who needs to forfeit our respect. Probably nobody knows much about the quality of the relationship between any man and any woman except the persons who have participated in it, and there would be much less misery in the world and, I believe, quite as much decency if other people could persuade themselves to avoid passing judgment on such relationships. Of course the Dickens marital smashup was a pitiful thing. Of course both Catherine and Dickens suffered deeply. One does not need to accept the sacramental view of marriage to believe that any decent person must suffer deeply at such a time. The breaking of ties even when they have galled unbearably, the painful sense of disloyalty and inadequacy that supervenes, the pitiful discrepancy between what this marriage promised and what it has delivered—all this adds up to about as hot a hell as human beings can be asked to go through in this life. But there are times when it must be faced, and I believe this was the situation that the Dickenses confronted.[49]

[49] Nobody doubts that Mrs. Dickens conducted herself with admirable dignity after the separation, but in one respect her situation was less difficult than that of Dickens and more conducive to dignity: she was not under accusation. To do her justice it is not necessary to assume that she saw the case with complete clarity, any more than Dickens did. However good a woman she was,

44

The presence of Ellen Ternan's name in Dickens's will (she is the very first person named in it, and he left her £1,000, free of legacy duty) is puzzling in any case, but a priori it seems to me to militate against the hypothesis of a guilty relationship rather than for it. Out of a £93,000 estate, £1,000 was a pleasant legacy to leave a dear young friend, but it would be a very niggardly bequest to a woman who, outside the protection of marriage, had given an older man her youth. "But, of course," say the skeptics, "he had provided for her privately." This may well be so, but why, then, mention her in the will at all, involving a permanent legal record of the bequest? And would John Forster have printed the will in the authorized biography of the novelist, with the knowledge and consent of the Dickens family, if all these persons knew that the very first person mentioned in it was the dead man's paramour? It is all very well to reply that a will is a public document and that

she may still have had all the shortcomings he attributed to her, and he may have been telling the exact truth when he said that the trouble between them began as far back as the time of Mamie's birth (when Ellen Ternan had not yet been conceived), and that she had often suggested a separation. She wanted Dickens's letters to her published (Walter Dexter, ed., *Mr. and Mrs. Charles Dickens: His Letters to Her* [Constable, 1935]) because she wanted the world to know that he had loved her, but when Mrs. Perugini read them she could not feel that they showed this. At the very least, I think we must admit that he had trouble with her, and condescended to her, as if she had been a child or a mental defective, even before their marriage (cf. J. W. T. Ley's review of the letters, *Dickensian*, Vol. XXXI [1935], 226–30). One puzzle involved in the interpretation of her character is the contrast between the placidity or sluggishness which seems so to have annoyed Dickens and the petulance or ill temper which we know her to have displayed during their courtship. As for Hebe Elsna's recent writings on the subject, all that needs to be said is that her first book, *Consider These Women* (Robert Hale, 1954) was published as a work of fiction, and that her second, *Unwanted Wife: A Defence of Mrs. Charles Dickens* (Jarrolds, 1963) ought to have sailed under the same flag. See Pansy Pakenham's temperate and discriminating review, *Dickensian*, Vol. LIX (1963), 125–28.

45

anybody who pays the necessary fee can consult it, but surely no-body is silly enough to believe that the public in general ever does anything like this, the book-buying public, that is, which reads Dickens's novels and Forster's biography.

If Ellen Ternan's life was "spoiled" by her association with Dickens to such an extent that she spent her later years a prey to remorse and finally confessed her "sin" to Canon Benham, then she must have been a far greater actress off the stage than she ever was on it. If we confine ourselves to what we know about her, and are willing to forget the wishful fantasies which diseased imaginations have conjured up, we get the picture of a serious, sincere, hard-working, loving, faithful, high-minded woman of strict principles, like her mother before her.[50] From 1876 on she was her husband's assistant in his professional work, and the way was never easy for either of them. He died in 1910. She succumbed in 1914 to the same dreadful malady that carried off Mrs. Dickens— cancer. Her daughter has no recollection of having been brought up by a Lady Dedlock. Ellen Ternan Robinson cherished her memories of her great friend, spoke of him freely and uncon-strainedly, on occasion gave "readings" from his works, and brought up her children to revere his name. She was on terms of intimate friendship with Mamie Dickens and Georgina Hogarth. Fortunately she was dead by the time the carrion-hunters got busy

[50] In "Ellen Ternan—Some Letters," *The Dickensian*, Vol. LXI (1965), 30–35, Leslie C. Staples published some newly discovered letters of Ellen Ternan to the distinguished Victorian publisher, George Smith. Relating as they do to an occasion in 1872 when she acted as a kind of unofficial literary agent for Alfred Austin, they have nothing to do with Dickens, but they do reveal a very intelligent, strong, and exceptionally straightforward woman. Smith behaves petulantly in comparison. Yes, whatever else she may have been wrong about, Mrs. Perugini was quite right when she said that Ellen Ternan had brains.

with her, but the sisters of her old nurse and companion, and later children's nurse, Jane Wheeler, were still alive, and they sent this message to Ellen's daughter, Gladys Reece: "Tell Gladys, if she ever asks, that I never mentioned the matter to her because it could only cause her pain, but that if she had asked me, I should have been able to say that her dear mother was never the mistress of Charles Dickens." "But, of course," say the skeptics, "Jane Wheeler would not really know." Perhaps not. Certainly her statement does not "prove" anything. But I still think she knew considerably more than Thomas Wright, Gladys Storey, Ada Nisbet, or Felix Aylmer.

If divorce had been possible for Dickens,[51] perhaps he and Ellen Ternan might have married. I do not know about that. It *may be* that, divorce being impossible, they finally established an extralegal union. I do not know about that either. If they did, I do not feel called upon either to justify them or to condemn them. I have said that, in some sense of the word, I am sure Dickens loved Ellen Ternan, and I will add that whatever they may have done, I am sure that what he felt for her was love and not lust. The fact that the tie, whatever it was, lasted until death severed it would alone show that. Moreover, everything that we know of Dickens shows that, susceptible as he was to the charm of women, he was incapable of being attracted by a woman who could not inflame his imagination to the extent of causing him to idealize her; even Kingsmill grants that he was "primarily a poet not a sensualist in his feeling for women." Mr. Aylmer argues that he did not profess

---

[51] It has been said that Dickens could have been divorced. Legally, yes. Practically, no. He would have had to be willing to be publicly branded for adultery plus either cruelty or desertion, and this would, in his position, have been out of the question. Moreover, how do we know that Mrs. Dickens would have agreed to a divorce?

"strict views on domestic morality" but cites no opinion except that he did not advocate "the maintenance of an unhappy marriage." If this is to be the criterion, then John Milton himself was a man of very loose morals. If, after years of struggle with herself or with him, Ellen Ternan finally gave him during his last years the "dear friend and companion" he had sought so long, then I, for one, am willing to grant that that was her business and that she was a better judge of the propriety of her action than we can ever be. As for Dickens, he can speak for himself, more eloquently than any of us can speak for him, nor has he ever ceased to do so:

> Though I have unquestionably suffered deeply from being lied about with a wonderful recklessness, I am not so weak or wrong-headed as to be in the least changed by it. I know the world to have just as much good in it as it had before; and no one has better reason to thank God for the friendship it contains, than I have. So I hope to regain my composure in a steady manner, and to live to be good and true to the innocent people who have been traduced along with me.[52]

And again:

> I know very well that a man who has won a very conspicuous position, has incurred in the winning of it, a heavy debt to the knaves and fools, which he must be content to pay, over and over again, all through his life. . . . I have been heavily wounded, but I have covered the wound up, and left it to heal. . . . And I hope that my books will speak for themselves and me, when I and my faults and virtues, my fortunes and misfortunes are all forgotten.[53]

[52] To Rev. Edward Tagart, June 14, 1858. "Nonesuch" Letters, III, 27.
[53] To W. F. de Cerjat, July 7, 1858. "Nonesuch" Letters, III, 29.

As of 1965, there is nothing that is known, or can reasonably be conjectured, concerning the Dickens-Ternan relationship that should make any sensible person doubt that Ellen Ternan was a respectworthy woman and Charles Dickens a respectworthy man.[54]

[54] Postscript. When the above was written, I had not yet seen Ada Nisbet's Dickens bibliography, in Lionel Stevenson, ed., *Victorian Fiction* (Harvard University Press, 1964). I must say that her attitude toward the Ternan matter seems to me somewhat more judicious here than it has hitherto been, though I cannot help being amused by the fact that though she herself told the world that she wrote *Dickens and Ellen Ternan* to reply to me, she carefully omits all mention of me, and of my articles on the subject in her account of the controversy!

Dickens at Work:
The Chimes

THE ENORMOUS VOGUE OF *A Christmas Carol* has probably served, in a measure at least, to draw the attention of at least the casual reader away from the fact that Dickens wrote four other Christmas books on a similar plan. I do not claim that *The Chimes* is worthy to stand beside the incomparable *Carol*. I do not even think it attains the stature of *The Cricket on the Hearth*. But it does happen to afford an unusually interesting test case for the contemplation of Dickens as both artist and prophet: first, because we know more about the circumstances of its genesis and growth than we do of many of his works; and, second, because its social and moral teaching is not only daring but interestingly anticipative of some more recent attitudes.

The Chimes was written in Genoa in 1844. This time Dickens began not with a story or a situation, but with an idea, a character, and a purpose. Just as, in writing *A Child's History of England*, he found it impossible to write about the past without importing all the problems and prejudices of the present into it, so now, during his Italian journey, he found it impossible, as he gazed upon foreign scenes, to withdraw his mind from a constant preoccupation with the problems of the London poor. "Ah!" he cried to Forster upon his return, describing the glories of Venice, "when I saw those places, how I thought that to leave one's hand upon the time, lastingly upon the time, with one tender touch for the mass of toiling people that nothing could obliterate, would be to lift oneself above the dust of all the Doges in their graves, and stand upon a giant's staircase that Sampson [*sic!*] couldn't overthrow!" The purpose, then, here as in the *Carol*, was to strike a blow for the poor, and never was Dickens more passionately sincere, never did he give stronger evidence of his astonishing capacity for complete surrender to the emotional appeal of the creatures of his own fancy than when he was writing this book.

The method of *The Chimes* differs widely, however, from that which he had used in the *Carol*. Here the protagonist, Scrooge, was an enemy of the poor, a man himself in comfortable circumstances, and the story, detailing his conversion, became in effect an appeal to the prosperous people of England, begging them to extend help and sympathy to those less fortunate than themselves. Implicitly, to be sure, this appeal inheres also in *The Chimes*. Indeed, at the very end it becomes explicit, in the author's direct appeal to the "listener," to "try to bear in mind the stern realities from which these shadows come; and in your sphere—none is too wide, and none too limited for such an end—endeavour to correct, improve, and soften them." But this is secondary. The principal character in *The Chimes* is the poverty-stricken ticket-porter, Toby Veck. He represents the poor themselves, not their oppressors, and it is as a symbol of the poor that he seems to Dickens to stand in need of conversion. Essentially the problem of *The Chimes* is a problem of faith—the individual's faith in himself and his ability to adjust to his world. Whatever else happens, Dickens seems to be saying, the poor must on no account be allowed to stop believing in themselves. Beauty and faithfulness and love are not incompatible with poverty; glee and merriment may even, on occasion, join hands with it. But once destroy the poor man's faith in himself and in the goodness of life, and there will be nothing left. Drunkenness, prostitution, arson, suicide, murder—all these must follow as the night the day.

In order to show that I have not misread his purpose, and to provide a basis for what is to follow, I must transcribe the following long sketch of how Dickens originally planned to develop *The Chimes*. It was sent, in a letter to his friend and future biographer John Forster, along with the First Quarter of the tale, in October, 1844:

> The general notion is this. That what happens to poor Trotty[1] in the first part, and what will happen to him in the second (when he takes the letter to a punctual and a great man of business, who is balancing his books and making up his accounts, and complacently expatiating on the necessity of clearing off every liability and obligation, and turning over a new leaf and starting fresh with the new year), so dispirits him, who can't do this, that he comes to the conclusion that his class and order have no business with a new year, and really are "intruding." And though he will pluck up for an hour or so, at the christening (I think) of a neighbour's child, that evening: still, when he goes home, Mr. Filer's precepts will come into his mind, and he will say to himself, "we are a long way past the proper average of children, and it has no business to be born": and will be wretched again. And going home, and sitting there alone, he will take that newspaper out of his pocket, and reading of the crimes and offences of the poor, especially of those whom Alderman Cute is going to put down, will be quite confirmed in his misgiving that they are bad; irredeemably bad. In this state of mind, he will fancy that the Chimes are calling to him; and saying to himself "God help me! Let me go up to 'em.
>
> [1] A nickname for Toby.

I feel as if I were going to die in despair—of a broken heart; let me die among the bells that have been a comfort to me!'"—will grope his way up into the tower; and fall down in a kind of swoon among them. Then the third quarter, in other words the beginning of the second half of the book, will open with the Goblin part of the thing: the bells ringing, and innumerable spirits (the sound or vibration of them) flitting and tearing in and out of the church-steeple, and bearing all sorts of missions and commissions and reminders and reproaches, and comfortable recollections and what not, to all sorts of people and places. Some bearing scourges; and others flowers, and birds, and music; and others pleasant faces in mirrors, and others ugly ones; the bells haunting people in the night (especially the last of the old year) according to their deeds. And the bells themselves, who have a goblin likeness to humanity in the midst of their proper shapes, and who shine in a light of their own, will say (the Great Bell being the chief spokesman): "Who is he that being of the poor doubts the right of poor men to the inheritance which Time reserves for them, and echoes an un-meaning cry against his fellows?" Toby, all aghast, will tell him it is he, and why it is. Then the spirits of the bells will bear him through the air to various scenes, charged with this trust: That they show him how the poor and wretched, at the worst—yes, even in the crimes that aldermen put down, and he has thought so horrible—have some deformed and hunchbacked goodness clinging to them; and how they have their right and share in Time. Following out the history of Meg, the Bells will show her, that marriage broken off and all friends dead, with an infant child; reduced so low, and made so miserable, as to be brought at last to wander out at night. And in Toby's sight, her father's, she will resolve to drown herself and the child together. But before she goes down to the water, Toby will see how she covers it with a part of her own wretched dress, and adjusts its rags so as to make it pretty in its sleep, and hangs over it, and smooths its little limbs, and loves it with the dearest love that God ever gave to mortal creatures; and when she runs down to the water, Toby will cry "Oh spare her! Chimes, have mercy on her! Stop her!"—and the bells will say, "Why stop her? She is bad at heart—let the bad die." And Toby on his knees will beg and pray for mercy: and in the end the bells will stop her, by their voices, just in time. Toby will see, too, what great things the punctual man has left undone on the close of the old year, and what accounts he has left unsettled: punctual as he is. And he will see a great many things about Richard, once so near being his son-in-law, and about a great many people. And the moral of it all will be, that he has his portion in the new year no less than any other man, and that the poor require a deal of beating out of shape before their human shape is gone; that even in their frantic wickedness, there may be good in their hearts triumphantly asserting itself, though all the aldermen alive say "No," as he has learnt from the agony of his own child; and that the truth is Trustfulness in them, not doubt, nor putting down, nor filing them away. And when at last a great sea rises, and this sea of Time comes sweeping down, bearing the alderman and such mudworms of the earth away to nothing, dashing them to fragments in its fury—Toby will climb a rock and hear the bells (now faded from his sight) pealing out upon the waters. And as he hears them, and looks round for help, he will wake up and find himself with the newspaper lying at his foot; and Meg sitting opposite to him at the table, and making up the ribbons for her wedding to-morrow; and the window open, that the sound of the bells ringing the old year out and the new year in may enter. They will just have broken out, joyfully; and Richard will dash in to kiss Meg before Toby, and have the first kiss of the new year (he'll get it too); and the neighbours will crowd round with good wishes; and a band will strike up gaily

(Toby knows a Drum in private); and the altered circumstances, and the ringing of the bells, and the jolly music, will so transport the old fellow that he will lead off a country dance forthwith in an entirely new step, consisting of his old familiar trot. Then quoth the inimitable[2]—Was it a dream of Toby's after all? Or is Toby but a dream? and Meg a dream? and all a dream! In reference to which, and the realities of which dreams are born, the inimitable will be wiser than he can be now, writing for dear life, with the post just going, and the brave C. booted. . . . Ah how I hate myself, my dear fellow, for this lame and halting outline of the Vision I have in mind. But it must go to you. . . . You will say what is best for the frontispiece.

Forster himself pointed out some of the principal differences between this first sketch and the story as it was written: "Fern the farm-labourer is not here, nor yet his niece the little Lilian (at first called Jessie), who is to give the tale its most tragical scene; and there are intimations of poetic fancy at the close of my sketch which the published story fell short of." Other differences remain to be noted. For example, the story as it now stands leaves no place for the christening of the neighbor's child which was first intended to occupy Toby's New Year's Eve; and the contemplated exposure of Sir Joseph Bowley has been omitted altogether. But the most striking and important change is that in the published version the Chimes do *not* intervene to save Meg from infanticide and self-destruction.

For all these changes the Ferns are directly responsible. When Toby unexpectedly took them into his house, it immediately became impossible for him to spend the evening with his neighbors. Dickens seems to have stumbled across them in the dark quite as

2 Dickens's whimsical name for himself.

suddenly as Toby himself did, and when they entered the story, they brought tragedy with them. The writer's mood seems now to have changed; he became more and more earnest, more and more relentless. He did not abandon his plan for the conversion of Toby, but in his most serious moments, he found himself thinking, more and more, of others. "You comfortable ones," one can almost hear him say, "you who regard the outcasts of the world as outcasts by choice, inferior creatures, evil to the heart's core. I will show you a child, an innocent, lovable child who will awaken all your sympathies. Then, virtually without preparation, I will plunge her, almost simultaneously, into girlhood and vice, and you who have loved her will not dare, as you read my pages, tell me that you would have done better in her place." And if Lilian were to be destroyed, why not Meg also? He would employ no last-minute rescue, no jot of supernatural melodrama: he would let them go— Meg and her child—they must die. Those readers of his who had shuddered with horror over newspaper stories of women killing their children: for once he would show them why women kill their children. He would show a Dickens heroine doing it, not because she was bad but because she was good, because she wanted to save her child from something worse than death. And Richard? Richard should not be a good and happy husband. Instead he should become a disillusioned drunkard and a criminal. For once Dickens would eschew romance: he would study relentlessly the forces that doom the poor to the destruction of their bodies and their souls. Why not?—since the moral could be made all the more powerful that way. And so, calamity having thus been piled upon calamity, the contemplated return to the earlier mood of the story and the reintroduction of Sir Joseph Bowley were seen to be impossible, and the apocalyptic splendors originally planned for were dropped as unnecessary and ineffective.

I have not forgotten that it is Dickens whose mood I am here attempting to reconstruct, and I am not unaware that all this seems —for him—somewhat bitter. But not any more bitter, I believe, than the story itself, and we have his own explicit testimony that his experience in writing it was very unusual.

> This book . . . has made my face white in a foreign land. My cheeks, which were beginning to fill out, have sunk again; my eyes have grown immensely large; my hair is very lank; and the head inside the hair is hot and giddy. Read the scene at the end of the third part, twice. I wouldn't write it twice for something. . . . Since I conceived, at the beginning of the second part, what must happen in the third, I have undergone as much sorrow and agitation as if the thing were real; and have wakened up with it at night. I was obliged to lock myself in when I finished it yesterday, for my face was swollen for the time to twice its proper size, and was hugely ridiculous.

Again:

> Third of November, 1844. Half-past two, afternoon. Thank God! I have finished *The Chimes*. This moment. I take up my pen again to-day, to say only that much; and to add that I have had what women call "a real good cry!"

Concerning Forster's own suggestions toward the improvement of the tale, while it was yet in the manuscript stage, the biographer has, as usual, told us little, though what details he does give are in this instance rather clearer and more definite than usual. "The red-faced gentleman with the blue coat" who appears in the First Quarter with Alderman Cute and Mr. Filer, we owe indirectly to Forster: he replaces a "Young England gentleman" to whom the biographer objected. It seems clear also that Forster softened Mr. Filer on the ground that, as Dickens had originally drawn him, he would offend the political economists, which, for that matter, he did, even as he now stands. "File away at Filer, as you please; but bear in mind that the *Westminster Review* considered Scrooge's presentation of the turkey to Bob Cratchit as grossly incompatible with political economy."

In the Preface to the "First Cheap Edition" of his *Christmas Books*, Dickens explained of all of them that "the narrow space within which it was necessary to confine these Christmas Stories when they were originally published, rendered their construction a matter of some difficulty, and almost necessitated what is peculiar in their machinery. I never attempted great elaboration of detail in the working out of character within such limits, believing that it could not succeed." The effect on characterization here alluded to will be considered later. Here let us glance at the effect on construction. As we have already seen, the end of *The Chimes* was not in sight from the beginning, but it did appear at a comparatively early stage. By the beginning of the Second Quarter the general outline was fixed and the space to be devoted to each portion at least roughly determined. The advantage of this careful planning may be judged by its results: *The Chimes* is, in every way, an admirably constructed story.

Especially skillful is the way the story opens. The First Quarter begins with an introductory paragraph in which, after earnestly declaring that "a story-teller and a story-reader should establish a mutual understanding as soon as possible," Dickens runs off into his usual burlesque style, and issues a mock-challenge to his readers, offering to meet all doubters, individually if need be, and thus demonstrate the unquestionable truth of his initial statement that "there are not many people . . . who would care to sleep in a church." There follows, in the second paragraph, the famous personified description of the Night Wind, always likely to be the most fearsome and awe-inspiring element in the experience of anyone who should attempt such a rash experiment. The third paragraph takes reader and Night Wind together "high up in the steeple," inevitably the most ghostly part of the church. Now that we are in the steeple, we are ready, of course, for the introduction of the Chimes themselves, the description of which occupies the fourth and fifth paragraphs. And then the principal character, Toby Veck, enters the story also, quite casually and incidentally.

In paragraphs six to eleven Toby is described—his character, his occupation, his station in life. Then, in paragraph twelve, Toby and the Chimes are clearly connected. First we are told about the old man's love for the bells; then the author goes into a fanciful elucidation of the "points of resemblance between themselves and him." In the thirteenth paragraph there is more about Toby's love for the Chimes, and of how "he invested them with a strange and solemn character." Nevertheless, he "scouted with indignation a certain flying rumor that the Chimes were haunted." Hereupon the introduction ends; Meg enters with Toby's dinner; the dramatic method is now employed; and the story proper may be said to have begun.

Now what has been accomplished so far? More, I think, than may as yet be apparent. The tone of the story has been determined and its principal character introduced and described. The very first statement of all—idle as it seems and whimsically as it is maintained ("There are not many people . . . who would care to sleep in a church")—has a certain suggestiveness in the way of foreshadowing, while the later insinuation of a "certain flying rumor that the Chimes were haunted" still further suggests the supernatural character of the tale. The air of weirdness may thus be said to predominate, but there are undertones which are quite as important. Thus, at the close of the second paragraph, we find this: "Ugh! Heaven preserve us, sitting round the fire!"—the appeal to the homing instinct and domestic comfort, always so characteristic of Dickens, the skillful suggestion that domestic comfort is to be an important part of the tale. A little later, the sympathetic quality of the Chimes is even more carefully suggested: they are "bent upon being heard on stormy nights, by some poor mother watching a sick child, or some lone wife whose husband was at sea." Then, the casual introduction of Toby Veck, as a kind of afterthought to the description of the Chimes themselves, suggests the curious way in which his life is to be bound up with them. Finally, this connection is made all the more inescapable by means of the comparison between Toby and the Chimes which has already been referred to.

It is not necessary to go through the entire story in such detail. But the element of careful preparation and foreshadowing is everywhere apparent. The first two quarters prepare carefully for the last two: all the elements which enter into Toby's waking life are given forth again, in new and hideous combinations, in his dream. Thus the dream is consistently presented to us *from Toby's own point of view.*

When he first appears before us, Toby is already a man whose faith in himself, in his class, and in life itself has been somewhat disturbed. There follows in quick succession a series of experiences all calculated to increase his doubts: Mr. Filer's demonstration that Toby himself is unpardonably past the average age, and that when he eats tripe he is stealing his food out of the mouths of widows and orphans; Alderman Cute's denunciation of Meg's desire to wed; Sir Joseph Bowley's horror that, unlike himself, Toby is not entering the New Year with a clean slate; finally, the hideous newspaper account of the poverty-stricken mother who has slain herself and her child. No one of these details is included idly. Each contributes to Toby's mood; each is to be used in working out the final resolution of the tale.

In the vision itself there are other careful bits of foreshadowing. Especially noteworthy for its delicate handling of a gross subject is the scene between Meg and Lilian in the Third Quarter, where we get the first hint that Lilian is to become a prostitute. Equally effective is Toby's repeated wondering, as he searches the throngs of his vision, concerning the whereabouts of Richard. In this way suspense is developed, and Richard's first appearance, dissipated and broken by hardship and disappointment, is made all the more impressive. The Chickenstalker episode, at the beginning of the Fourth Quarter, serves as legitimate comic relief, but it does more than that. It has a vital connection with the story, and the conversation between Mrs. Chickenstalker and Toby includes a careful summary of the various influences that have conspired to wreck Meg and Richard. Best of all is the use made of Meg's love for her child. " 'Thank God!' cried Trotty, holding up his folded hands. 'O God be thanked! She loves the child!' " But soon comes the warning voice: " 'Follow her!' was sounded through the house. 'Learn it from the creature dearest to your heart!' "

It would be interesting to know what were the original contents of the note which Toby carries to Sir Joseph Bowley. By the time this message is delivered, in the Second Quarter, Dickens has, as we have seen, made up his mind concerning the roles which Lilian and her uncle are to play in the working out of his story. But at the time the note is sent, this idea has not yet been developed. It is nevertheless entirely possible that the note may have been conceived originally just as it now stands—an expression of Alderman Cute's stern determination to put Will Fern down. Originally, we may suppose, the incident was intended simply to illustrate the characters of Cute and Bowley, and this before the idea had come to Dickens of introducing Will Fern into the story as anything more than a name. As the thing stands, it does illustrate perfectly both the obsequiousness of Cute and the impotent grandiloquence of Bowley; what other purpose could any other note, in this contingency, have served? It is probable, then, that when the idea of Lilian came to Dickens, he picked up this thread, and made the incident, originally a very minor one, a bit of preparation for more important matters.

Dickens's own opinion with regard to characterization in his *Christmas Books* has already been cited. In *The Chimes*, Toby alone is anything more than the suggestion of a character. There is no character development even in Toby. but there is progressive revelation of character, and this extends clear through the first half of the tale. Here it is dropped, and our attention is centered upon the vision. Toby is individualized through description, soliloquy, and dramatic scene. The crowning revelation of his character comes in the Second Quarter, when he offers shelter to Lilian and Will Fern.

The other serious characters can hardly be said to be characterized at all. Lilian must have been real in Dickens's imagination, or he could not have been so moved as he was by her fall, but he can hardly be said to have communicated a sense of her reality to the reader. For this reason, the scene at the end of the Third Quarter seems to me artistically ineffective, though its social implications are suggestive indeed. Alderman Cute, Mr. Filer, and Sir Joseph Bowley—though we catch hardly more than a glimpse of each—are far more vivid, much more real than Lilian, Meg, or Richard. Next to Toby himself, Sir Joseph is certainly the best character. His passion for entering the new year with all the obligations of the old behind him is a convenient "tag" of the kind Dickens could always use skillfully, but better still is his highly characteristic speech—his curious hesitancy, his hovering on the edge of pious generalities only to lapse immediately again into the mundane.

So much for the art of *The Chimes*; what now of its spirit? First of all, it has a definite affinity with the teachings of Carlyle. After finishing the story in Genoa, Dickens made a special trip to England to read it to a group of friends. "Shall I confess to you," he writes to Forster, "that I particularly want Carlyle above all to see it before the rest of the world?" The tale has often been criticized on the ground of Dickens's alleged ignorance of the real causes of social misery. Even the admiring E. P. Whipple wrote in this connection: "Now we must suppose that John Stuart Mill was a good and brave man, and that he had some love as well as perception of truth, yet certainly his opinion would have substantially agreed with that of Mr. Filer, so mercilessly ridiculed for his opposition to improvident marriages among the poor." This may or may not be true, but not all the naïveté was on one side. Surely if either Mill or Whipple seriously believed that marriages among the poor could be made to cease simply because they were "improvident," then these gentlemen were themselves much more naïve, much more "romantic" and unscientific, than Dickens, in his wildest flights of fancy, ever dreamed of being.

The most startling thing about *The Chimes*, however, is that here, in 1844, we find Dickens asserting without compromise that prostitution, drunkenness, murder, arson, and revolution come into the world, not because prostitutes, drunkards, revolutionists, and their kind are by nature viler than other human beings, and not because they love darkness better than light, but simply because, as our social order is constituted, some of its members never do get a fair chance for their share of the decencies of life. I do not pretend that Dickens would defend all his criminals thus; certainly no such plea could cover Fagin or Bill Sikes.[3] But this is unmistakably his teaching in *The Chimes*. Lilian becomes a prostitute because her soul is crushed by unrewarded toil; Richard, frightened away from marriage and domestic happiness by his poverty, sinks lower and lower into drunkenness and sloth until at last he revenges himself upon society as a revolutionary firebrand; Meg slays her child to obviate the possibility that she may live to follow in Lilian's footsteps. And in every case, says Dickens, it is society, not these poor outcasts, that is to blame.

It must have been startling beyond belief in 1844, so startling that probably not many readers grasped all its implications. If they had, the matter could hardly have been permitted to pass off so quietly. For, on a broader scale, Dickens here lays down precisely the same principle which Bernard Shaw was to enunciate

[3] In *Dickens and Crime* (London, Macmillan, 1962), Philip Collins shows, among other things, that Dickens's attitude toward crime and criminals, especially in later life, so far from being sentimental, was, in some aspects, what we would call really savage.

with reference to prostitution at the close of the century. Listen to Shaw's defense of *Mrs. Warren's Profession*:

> The play is, simply, a study in prostitution, and its aim is to show that prostitution is not the prostitute's fault, but the fault of a society which pays for a poor and pretty woman's prostitution in solid gold, and pays for her honesty with starvation, drudgery, and pious twaddle.

It is surely not necessary to enlarge here on the consternation with which *Mrs. Warren's Profession* was greeted well into the twentieth century. In some cases, the anxiety went to the length of expressing itself in police prosecution. William Winter, dean of American drama critics, saw in this play and others like it the overthrow of whatever was pure, lovely, and of good report in the theater.

The case of Richard has a definite bearing also on the much-mooted matter of Dickens's sentimentalism. In Toby's dream, Meg and Richard do finally marry, but they marry too late. As Mrs. Chickenstalker explains it to Toby: "He went on better for a short time; but his habits were too old and strong to be got rid of; he soon fell back a little; and was falling fast back, when his illness came so strong upon him." And even as she speaks, the word comes that Richard has passed away.

Now if there is anything characteristic of the sentimentalist, it is the belief that good resolutions can effect anything. It is notable, and it should be considered in the discussion of Dickens, that in this case good resolutions accomplish precisely nothing. As irrevocably as any determinist today, Dickens says: It is too late. The die is cast. Richard must perish.

But there is still another aspect of the story which we have not

65

yet considered, and whose consideration may bring us closer to anything that has been said thus far to the secret of Dickens's art. It must be remembered that all the terrible things of which I have spoken take place in a dream. When Toby wakes up, it is to learn that Meg is going ahead with her wedding plans in spite of Alderman Cute, and the story ends in general festivity and merry-making. The enemy of Dickens points triumphantly to this circumstance as an example of the novelist's shallowness and cowardice. When he did face the realities of life, it was only in a dream! Dreams are realities in his world, and realities have become dreams. We close in a stifling atmosphere of bourgeois respectability. But let us see.

It must be admitted that out-and-out realism was not the fashion in Dickens's day, and great writers, as well as small ones, are conditioned by literary fashion. This is nowhere more evident than among those who object to Dickens's alleged optimism: they are simply following the pessimistic, naturalistic trend of *their* day! If they would really be independent and original, let them turn to romance. It would be far more audacious, in this year of grace, to write like Dickens (if they could!) than to write like Gorky. But a dream within a dream can hardly be considered, in any appreciable degree, more unreal than the dream itself. The whole story of *The Chimes* exists in the imagination: that which Toby dreams is quite as vividly presented as that which actually happens to him, and he who pretends that it would take a very brave man to present these things as having actually happened while any coward might present them as dreams, has surely forgotten that he is dealing, not with life, but with a work of fiction. Finally, it may be urged, the exigencies of his plan and purpose compelled Dickens to use the method he chose. The theme of the story was the restoration of Toby's faith in himself and his class. Following as it did in the wake of *A Christmas Carol*, supernatural machinery was absolutely necessary. Toby, like Scrooge, sees in a dream the dark road whither he is tending: he wakens with relief and turns his feet in another direction.

Dickens may very well have believed that something like that actually could be effected in human experience. He was no wide-eyed innocent during his later years, and the atmosphere of some of the last novels is pretty somber. But he never became a futili-tarian, and though he may have felt at times that he had lost the way, he always knew that there was a way. It is here, I think, that we touch the prime difference between Dickens and many con-temporary writers. He saw evil quite as clearly as they do, and he was quite as courageous, but, unlike many of them, he had retained faith. And by this I do not mean faith in God merely (though that is involved in it) but faith in humanity and in the world's destiny. Consequently, where they deal in fears and despairs, he deals in hopes and promises. Consequently (though I assert no parity with Dante), his work is a great comedy, not a great tragedy.

G. K. Chesterton had much to say on this point in connection with his inquiry as to why it was that "this too easily contented Dickens, this man with cushions at his back and (it sometimes seems) cotton wool in his ears, this happy dreamer, this vulgar optimist . . . alone among modern writers did really destroy some of the wrongs he hated and bring about some of the reforms he desired."[4] And he went on to answer his own question in words that are beautifully illustrated in *The Chimes*:

And the reason of this is one that goes deep into Dickens's

[4] Later investigation would seem to indicate that Chesterton considerably exaggerated Dickens's influence upon reform.

social reform, and, like every other real and desirable thing, involves a kind of mystical contradiction. If we are to save the oppressed, we must have two apparently antagonistic emotions in us at the same time. We must think the oppressed man immensely miserable, and, at the same time, intensely attractive and important. We must insist with violence upon his degradation; we must insist with the same violence upon his dignity. For if we relax by one inch the one assertion, men will say he does not need saving. And if we relax by one inch the other assertion, men will say he is not worth saving. . . .

Out of this perennial contradiction arises the fact that there are always two types of the reformer. The first we may call for convenience the pessimistic, the second the optimistic reformer. One dwells upon the fact that souls are being lost; the other dwells upon the fact that they are worth saving. . . . The first describes how bad men are under bad conditions. The second describes how good men are under bad conditions.

There is much more to the same effect that I have not space to quote. Now turn, for illustration of the other method, to the suggestive analysis of Van Wyck Brooks (in *Emerson and Others*) of the reasons for what he considers Upton Sinclair's failure as a social reformer through fiction:

But suppose now, that one wishes to see the dispossessed rise in their might and really, in the name of justice, take possession of the world. Suppose one wishes to see the class-system abolished, along with all the other unhappy things that Mr. Sinclair writes about. This is Mr. Sinclair's own desire; and he honestly believes that in writing as he does he contributes to this happy consummation. I cannot agree with him. In so far as Mr. Sinclair's books show anything real they show us the utter helplessness, the benightedness, the naïveté of the American workers' movement. Jimmie Higgins does not exist as a character. He is a symbol, however, and one can read reality into him. He is the American worker incarnate. Well, was there ever a worker so little the master of his fate? That, in point of fact, is just the conclusion Mr. Sinclair wishes us to draw. But why is he so helpless? Because, for all his kindness and his courage, he is, from an intellectual and social point of view, unlike the English worker, the German, Italian, Russian, the merest infant; he knows nothing about life or human nature or economics or philosophy or even his enemies. How can he possibly set about advancing his own cause, how can he circumvent the wily patrioteers, how can he become anything but what he is, the mere football of everyone who knows more than he? Let us drop the "cultivated-class" standpoint and judge Mr. Sinclair's novels from the standpoint of the proletariat itself. They arouse the emotion of self-pity. Does that stimulate the worker or does it merely "console" him? They arouse the emotion of hatred. Does that teach him how to grapple with his oppressors or does it place him all the more at his oppressors' mercy? The most elementary knowledge of human nature tells us that there is only one answer to these questions.

With the justice or injustice of Brooks's evaluation of Upton Sinclair, I am not here concerned. The interesting thing is his substantial agreement with Chesterton that the pessimistic reformer is ineffective. Perhaps, after all, it was not mere cowardice and love of middle-class creature comfort that led Dickens to use humor and optimism in his pictures of the poor.

I began this study of *The Chimes* with the statement that it afforded a test case for the study of Dickens. The nineteenth century is not yet very far from us in point of time; it would not seem that any great feat of orientation must be performed in order to understand it. Yet if, as the advocates of the millennium assure us, we now move more rapidly in fifty years than we used to travel through the course of centuries, then it may well be necessary, now and then, to check up on our prepossessions to avoid the danger of judging nineteenth-century writers by their standards rather than our own. Many of the unfavorable judgments of Dickens that were in vogue some years ago, when he was less in fashion than he is at present, were, it seems to me, determined by failure to observe this caution, though I should hesitate to say that when we differ from him, the reason must be that we are right while he is wrong. Perhaps the most penetrating of all Chesterton's wise observations was that our time is a time, not the Day of Judgment.

Dickens in Longfellow's Letters and Journals

I

LONGFELLOW FIRST MET DICKENS in January, 1842, upon the novelist's first visit to Boston, and he accepted him at once as "a glorious fellow"—"a gay, free-and-easy character, with a fine bright face, blue eyes, and long dark hair, and withal a slight dash of the Dick Swiveller about him."[1] It is interesting that both here and in London, where he visited Dickens before the year was out, Longfellow's admiration embraced Mrs. Dickens also: "a good-natured—mild, rosy young woman—not beautiful, but amiable."[2] There is no suggestion that he sensed any incompatability between her and her husband.

Dickens's resemblance to Dick Swiveller was not passed over so lightly by Longfellow's youngest brother, later the Reverend Samuel Longfellow, a distinguished Unitarian clergyman and the poet's biographer. "Sam," as the family called him, reported as follows to his sister, Mrs. James Greenleaf, in New Orleans:

You have already heard about Dickens's arrival in Boston &

[1] MS: HWL (Henry Wadsworth Longfellow), Letter to his father, Jan. 30, 1842. This paper is a by-product of the author's research for *Longfellow: A Full-Length Portrait* and *Mrs. Longfellow: Selected Letters and Journals* (Longmans, Green, 1955, 1956). Except where otherwise indicated, quotations from manuscript material are by kind permission of the Longfellow Trustees and the Harvard College Library.

[2] MS: HWL, Journal, Jan. 30, 1842.

will have read, perhaps, the report of the young men's dinner, which was the most elegant & delightful ever known in Boston. Boston has been in a great toss but as he left on Saturday has by this time recovered a portion of its wonted propriety. I had the pleasure of seeing Dickens, nay of breakfasting with him at Henry's on Friday, at 10½ o'clock. I confess I did not find him quite my ideal Boz. He is very animated and talkative, pleasant but not particularly humorous, with an offhand way, and the slightest possible tincture of rowdyism in his appearance. He is the man who wrote Dick Swiveller & Pickwick drunk or something a little better than that—but not the creator of Oliver Twist & Little Nell. He has none of that refinement and scholarly look which we are apt to attach to our idea of a literary man; in other words he is just what we ought to expect when we recollect his history instead of his books. His hair is long, combed by his fingers & apparently guiltless of all acquaintance with a brush, in short not neat. His face is agreeable not so handsome as, tho' somewhat resembling the large lithograph which Henry has. His features are in constant play while he talks, particularly his eyebrows, giving him a French aspect. He speaks fast & rather indistinctly, reminding me of Horatio Smith, when he does not stutter. I sat opposite to him between Andrews Norton & Pierce; Sumner, Felton & Sam Ward completed the party. He talked about the literary people of England, & told us of Mrs. Norton being allowed at last to see her children. She went one day to her lawyer's, Mr. Proctor's, & found him playing with his children. He was so much moved by the feelings she exhibited that he promised her that by some means or other she should see her children. She said that every morning when she woke she felt that they were one day nearer forgetting their mother forever. Sumner spoke of her having several years ago assisted a young friend to elope which was thought rather against her. "Yes," said Dickens, "she made the night caps, and it was natural enough too in a young person. I'm sure I should be very happy to help anybody run away." He said that Quilp was entirely a creature of the imagination he had heaped together in him all possible hideousness. Pierce told him however of a real Quilp, at Salem, with wife, mother-in-law & all. I should have mentioned to you that he hadn't been in the room three minutes before Sumner took him to the window—it was open—& showing him the view seized the book & began to read River that in silence windest, when Henry rushed up and put a stop to the proceeding. The river Charles never looked more unpoetical. It was a cloudy day—the tide was down the hills were black and the meadows dirty.—Mr. Worcester came in just at the close & told Boz that the house was Washington's H.Q., of which he had been already twice informed by Sumner and Mr. Norton; and as they were going down stairs, Joey beckoned to him curiously & said, Here, won't you step into my parlor a minute—he went in & was introduced to Mrs. W & Miss Charlotte and somebody else who was there for the purpose. By the by Miss Maria Fay & the fair one had contrived accidentally to call upon Mrs. Worcester about half-past ten & were I presume sitting at the window when Dickens came in. As Miss Charlotte remarked, it might perhaps be considered a pardonable curiosity. From Henry's the distinguished stranger went to call upon the President [of Harvard College], stopping on his way at the Printing Office (!) The Pres. of course took him to the Library, where were assembled a small crowd of admiring boys & young ladies, such as the Higginsons & the two above named; thence he walked by easy stages to Mr. Sparks', stopping at Tutor Wheeler's that he might see a student's room, at Sumner's suggestion—& finally went into town in a carriage with said Sumner, an umbrella, a bear skin coat, & two octavo volumes of Longfellow's poems.[3]

[3] MS: Samuel Longfellow, Letter to Mrs. James Greenleaf, Feb. 8, 1842.

Three days before this letter was written, Richard Henry Dana, author of *Two Years Before the Mast*, wrote William Cullen Bryant in New York, to prepare him for Dickens's visit to that city:

> ... He *is very desirous of seeing you.* The very first sight of him may not wholly please you. But that will pass off in a moment, & if you do not greatly *take to him*, I am much mistaken. He is full of life. And with him life does not appear to be according to the Brunonian theory a forced state—but a truly *natural* one. I never saw a face fuller of vivid action, or an eye fuller of light. And he is so freely animated—so unlike *our folks.* He is plainly enough a most hearty man, & a most kind hearted one. People do not seem to crowd about him as to see a lion, but from downright love of him:—As Richard said to me—you can't bear to leave him.[4]

Dickens's warmest admirer among the Boston literati, however, was probably Cornelius Conway Felton, professor of Greek at Harvard, and later president of the College. While Dickens was still in Boston he defended him twice against the strictures and reservations of Andrews Norton (the "Pope of Unitarianism") and his wife, parents of Charles Eliot Norton:

> ... In the evening Longfellow and I went to Mr. Norton's; I had a dispute with Mr. and Mrs. N. about Dickens. They maintained that he showed but little knowledge of human nature, and I that his knowledge was profound and exact. Mr. Norton affirmed that such a character as Oliver Twist was an impossibility, and gave many reasons for that opinion. I maintained that the character was not only beautiful but true in the highest degree to nature. Neither convinced the other, and neither yielded a jot.

[4] MS: Richard Henry Dana, Letter to William Cullen Bryant, Feb. 5, 1842 (Courtesy, Massachusetts Historical Society).

And again, upon another visit:

> . . . Mrs. N. was speaking with wonder of the enthusiasm with
> which Dickens is regarded and received. She said she was not
> surprised that his books should be liked. They were well, some of
> them *very well*. I replied, that I thought the kindliness and hu-
> manity displayed in his works, sufficiently accounted for his per-
> sonal popularity. That everybody felt he was a *good fellow*, and
> as to his books being well, or *very well*, I had been convinced since
> the first number of Pickwick, that one of the greatest minds of the
> age was coming out, and that I now entertained a profound con-
> viction that Dickens was the most original and inventive genius
> since Shakespeare! What do you say to that? Am I not more than
> half right?[5]

Felton was in New York during Dickens's visit there, and on
February 22, Sam Ward (Julia Ward Howe's brother) wrote
Longfellow that Felton and the novelist had been together "daily
and almost hourly":

> . . . They have walked, laughed, talked, eaten oysters and drunk
> champagne together until they have almost grown together—in
> fact nothing but the interference of Madame D—— prevented
> their being attached to each other like the Siamese Twins, *a vol-
> ume of Pickwick serving as connecting membrane.* Imagine them
> strolling up Broadway—the grave Eliot Professor and the *Swell-
> ing*, theatrical Boz—the little man with the red waistcoat—talking
> Pickwickian and Barnaby—and those meeting them doubting
> that their minutest peculiarities of aspect were inscribed as rapidly
> as they were reflected in the Daguerreotype retina of Dickens's
> eye.[6]

[5] MS: Cornelius C. Felton, Letter to Henry R. Cleveland, Jan. 24, 1842.
[6] MS: Sam Ward, Letter to HWL, Feb. 22, 1842.

Nearly three months afterwards, Longfellow's wife-to-be, Fanny Appleton, reported to her brother, Thomas G. Appleton, of having heard their friend, Charles Sumner, read a letter which Dickens had written Felton:

> in the true Pickwickian vein in regard to the delights of oyster cellars, & his affection for his household gods even to the bars on his cook's cap, but very unlike that amiable & much-enduring personage in the indignation at our thievish booksellers. This book [i.e., *Martin Chuzzlewit*] will apparently be far from what is expected jocose & good natured, but is to lash our backs again about copyright & slavery. He meant, what would have been far wiser, only to introduce his American experiences to spice his future sketches of humanity, but his friends choose to expect a book about us which is very stupid of them, I think, for it is a thrice told tale & not in his line.[7]

From New York Dickens himself sent Longfellow an invitation to visit him in London. The poet was so delighted that he copied the entire letter, including a very fair imitation of Dickens's signature, and sent it to his father on February 27.

The primary object of Longfellow's journey was to take the "water-cure" in Germany. Before sailing, late in April, he wrote Sumner from New York:

> I have been this evening to see a play called *Boz*. It is a caricature on Dickens's reception here. Dickens is very well represented by Horncastle. The best joke in the piece is the invitation from the members of an Engine Company to see a fire, and the accompanying request to know whether he will have a single house burnt, or a whole block. He is also invited to see a steamer

[7] MS: FEA (Fanny Elizabeth Appleton), Letter to Thomas G. Appleton, June 14, 1842.

burst her boiler on the North River! I tried exceedingly hard to amuse myself; but found it rather dull.[8]

On September 17 Longfellow wrote the same correspondent from abroad: "I have entirely, *entirely* recovered from that attack of *anti-English* spleen; and promise myself great pleasure from my visit to Dickens."[9] The visit materialized in October, and seems to have been greatly enjoyed by both parties. The letter which Dickens sent Longfellow from Broadstairs, September 28, when he was afraid that he might have missed his visit through absence from home, is in quite his liveliest vein, but is too well known to be reprinted here.[10] From Dickens's study Longfellow sent Sumner, on October 16, his impressions of *American Notes.* "It is jovial and good-natured, and at times very severe. You will read it with delight and, for the most part, approbation."[11] Writing to John Forster early in 1843, Longfellow sends kisses to all the Dickens children, and especially to "noble little Charlie," "fine little Charlie, whom I can now see as distinctly as if he were standing before me."[12]

II

Longfellow and Dickens did not meet again until the novelist came to Boston late in 1867 on his famous American reading tour. Correspondence had apparently done little or nothing to bridge the gap of years. It seems strange that Longfellow should have

[8] MS: HWL, Letter to Charles Sumner, Apr. 26, 1842.
[9] MS: HWL, Letter to Charles Sumner, Sept. 17, 1842.
[10] Cf. Samuel Longfellow, *Life of Henry Wadsworth Longfellow* (Ticknor and Company, 1886), I, 18–19.
[11] *Ibid.*, I, 421.
[12] MS: HWL, Letters to John Forster, Feb. 28, May 24, 1843.

written so much more to Forster than he did to Dickens.[13] But, like all the rest of the world, the poet and his circle were diligently reading and commenting upon Dickens's various books as they appeared.

Longfellow did not always admire. As already indicated, he accepted the strictures contained in the *American Notes* with good grace, and it does not seem that his comment on *Pictures from Italy* as "all drollery" while Goethe on the same subject was "all wisdom" was meant to be slighting, for he also calls the volume "the finest and the funniest" book of travels he ever read.[14] To Felton he writes, "Dickens's description of Genoa makes me quite crazy. If I were rich enough, I would give my Professorship 'a punch in the head,' and retire to Italy forthwith."[15] But the novels themselves drew mixed notices. *Martin Chuzzlewit, Dombey and Son,* and *Little Dorrit* were the ones with which he was most inclined to find fault, while he greatly admired *David Copperfield, Bleak House,* and *The Mystery of Edwin Drood.*

Having received the third number of *Chuzzlewit,* he wrote Forster that "The story opens with great freshness and vigor," giving special praise, among other things, to "The Autumn Evening," "Tom Pinch's journey to Salisbury," and "the great, moral Pecksniff."[16] But the letter he sent his father a month later compels us to choose between believing that he had changed his opinion during the interval or that the earlier letter was not quite a frank or full expression of his mind. "Shall I send you the numbers of Dickens's new book, Chuzzlewit?" he asks. "I do not think

[13] Longfellow's letters to Forster are in the Victoria and Albert Museum, London, who have graciously consented to my quoting from them in this article.
[14] Samuel Longfellow, *Life*, II, 44.
[15] MS: HWL, Letter to C. C. Felton, Apr., 1846.
[16] MS: HWL, Letter to John Forster, Feb. 28, 1843.

it very amusing as yet, but it will no doubt grow better when he gets fully under way."[17]

Just after Christmas, 1847, he confides to his journal how "The evening whiled away with a new No. of Dombey, in which the proud Edith falls to pieces in the arms of Carker."[18] In March, 1848, he finds No. 17 "poor enough: mere filling up as it were."[19] Having finished the work, he records, late in April:

> The last two Nos. of Dombey. Heavy enough. No wonder; when one thinks that the author has gone through so many large octavo pages; more than six hundred. There is the trouble. Too much filling up:—writing against Time—or rather against space.[20]

He reread *Dombey* in 1861, but he still found it "a dismal book, though," he now adds, "rich in character and with a great deal of fun in it. . . . The description of Dr. Blimber's school is capital."[21]

Longfellow's enthusiasm for *David Copperfield* is reflected in his letter to Forster, December 7, 1851:

> It is very good news to hear that Dickens is beginning a new book. The last was a grand one; with a richer and deeper tone about it, than any of the others perhaps. Before this reaches you we shall be reading No. 1 of the new story.[22]

"The new story" was *Bleak House*, and it does not seem to have disappointed him, for in 1853 he speaks of it as "very exciting

[17] Samuel Longfellow, *Life*, II, 13.
[18] MS: HWL, Journal, Dec. 29, 1847.
[19] MS: HWL, Journal, Mar. 6, 1848.
[20] MS: HWL, Journal, Apr. 26, 1848.
[21] MS: HWL, Journal, Mar. 7, 1861.
[22] MS: HWL, Letter to John Forster, Dec. 7, 1851.

DICKENS AND THE SCANDALMONGERS

and interesting."[23] He began reading *Little Dorrit* in December, 1855;[24] the following March he had "another chapter" of it— "not so good as the last: and not helping the story on much."[25] In September, 1865, he records reading *Our Mutual Friend* but expresses no opinion.[26]

The most interesting comment on *A Tale of Two Cities* in the Longfellow papers comes from the older son, Charles Appleton Longfellow, who was not the most literary member of the family. On October 2, 1863, he wrote his sister Alice from Catlett's Station, Virginia, where he was encamped with the Union Army: "It has been raining all day, so that I have finished the 'Tale of Two Cities' it is first rate, isn't it?"[27]

As has already appeared in connection with *Dombey*, Longfellow sometimes reread Dickens's novels. Thus he comments upon *Barnaby Rudge* in 1860, when it was far from being a new book: "Dickens is always prodigal and ample; but what a set of vagabonds he contrives to introduce us to."[28] But by all means the most interesting comment on rereading is this on *Pickwick* from 1861:

> Afternoon and evening read "Pickwick"—It contains all Dickens in embryo, as an Overture does an Opera: themes and motives just touched upon, which are more elaborately developed in later works.[29]

[23] MS: HWL, Journal, Aug. 6, 1853.
[24] MS: HWL, Journal, Dec. 19, 1855.
[25] MS: HWL, Journal, Mar. 21, 1856.
[26] MS: HWL, Journal, Sept. 23, 1865.
[27] MS: Charles A. Longfellow, Letter to Alice M. Longfellow, Oct. 2, 1863.
[28] Samuel Longfellow, *Life*, II, 351.
[29] MS: HWL, Journal, Mar. 28, 1861.

The most interesting comments on the *Christmas Books* come from Mrs. Longfellow, who, naturally enough, is most enthusiastic about the *Carol*. She and Longfellow read it together after midnight of January 26–27, 1844, and she is presumably speaking for both of them when she calls it "an admirable performance with a true Xmas glow about it, yet very pathetic and poetical besides."[30] A few days later she goes into some detail, in a letter to her brother Tom:

> Have you seen Dickens' "Xmas Carol"? He sent it to Felton in its English garb, with capital wood cuts, & a nice clear type! It is a most admirable production I think, & has had great success in England, comforting people for the tediousness of Chuzzlewit. It is evidently written at *heat* from the *heart*, & has a Xmas crackle & glow about it, besides much pathos & poetry of conception, which form a rich combination. The sketch of the poor clerk's dinner is in his best manner, & almost consoles one for the poverty it reveals.[31]

Two years later she finds "Dickens' laughable & pathetic 'Cricket on the Hearth' . . . a kind of entremet to Carlyle's Cromwell," which her tendencies towards pacifism do not help her to enjoy.[32] She strikes the same note in her comment on another Christmas Book in 1847:

> Dickens's "Battle of Life" shows he is waking up with the rest of the world to a knowledge of the truly honorable victories— & can distinguish between a hero & a butcher.[33]

[30] MS: FEAL (Fanny E. Appleton Longfellow), Journal, Jan. 27, 1844.
[31] MS: FEAL, Letter to Thomas G. Appleton, Jan. 31, 1844.
[32] MS: FEAL, Letter to Emmeline Wadsworth, Jan. 28, 1846.
[33] MS: FEAL, Letter to Thomas G. Appleton, Jan. 31, 1847.

On January 8, 1849, Longfellow himself read the first half of *The Haunted Man* but found it "rather tedious."[34]

The Longfellows quoted freely from Dickens's novels also, and they were sufficiently familiar with his characters to be frequently reminded of them by persons and incidents encountered in their own lives. In a journal Longfellow wrote for his son Charley when he was small, he records buying him a wooden toy, "a man in black turning a crank. Papa called him 'Mr. Mantalini with his mangle.' "[35] In much more serious vein, he seems to have been greatly impressed by the passage on death and immortality which Dickens writes at the death of Paul Dombey. This he copied into his "Index Rerum" under "Death," and he quotes from it again in a letter to Robert Winthrop:

> I was this morning at the rooms of the Historical Society. The sun was shining pleasantly in at the window; beneath was the churchyard, reminding me of that "old, old fashion, Death"; and within, the busts, and pictures and books, suggesting the still "older fashion, Immortality."[36]

The serious and the jocular are nicely mingled in an 1872 letter to George Washington Greene, in which Longfellow says that Dante's lines,

> *collecto risponde*
> *Senza chiamare, e grida: io mi subbarco,*

would be in English, "Barkis is willing."[37]

---

[34] MS: HWL, Journal, Jan. 8, 1849.
[35] MS: HWL, Journal for Charles Longfellow, Apr. 3, 1850.
[36] MS: HWL, Letter to Robert C. Winthrop, May 8, 1868 (Courtesy, Massachusetts Historical Society).
[37] MS: HWL, Letter to George W. Greene, June 23, 1872.

Fanny Appleton played Mrs. Mantalini in tableaux presented at Lenox, Massachusetts, in 1839; Dickens tied with Shakespeare, furnishing the material for six out of the sixteen numbers presented. That same year an inn in the Berkshires reminded her of the one where Mr. Pickwick had his adventure with the lady in curlpapers.[38] In 1840 she reported having found her sister Mary and Mary's recently acquired husband looking "as happy as Miss La Creevy & Tim Linkinwater."[39] She quotes Sam Weller in an 1840 letter from Newport: "This is coming it rayther strong, as Sam Weller would say."[40] Much more interesting is the Dickensian reference in the first letter she wrote Longfellow's mother after becoming engaged to marry her son: "I have no right to be selfish in my days of abundance, but when will the heart be taught like poor Oliver Twist not to 'ask for *more*'?"[41] In a letter to her father, written soon after she and her husband had settled down at "Castle Craigie," as she liked to call the Craigie House, she compares their servant to Newman Noggs.[42] Twice her second son Ernest reminded her of Mr. Pickwick. Once was when he trotted about "as fast as a red spider, rolling his head like a Mandarin, & smiling with Pickwickian complacence."[43] Again, at a children's party, "Erny was as smiling as Mr. Pickwick & entered into it as heartily & genially as that angel in gaiters would have done."[44]

In 1856, when Samuel Longfellow had the jaundice, he spoke

[38] MS: FEA, Journal, Sept. 13, 1839.
[39] MS: FEA, Letter to Emmeline Austin, Jan. 5, 1840.
[40] MS: FEA, Letter to Emmeline Austin, July 6, 1840.
[41] MS: FEA, Letter to Zilpah Longfellow, May 27, 1843.
[42] MS: FEAL, Letter to her father, July 20, 1843.
[43] MS: FEAL, Letter to Anne Longfellow Pierce, Jan. 27, 1847.
[44] MS: FEAL, Letter to Samuel Longfellow, June 11, 1847.

of his malady in a letter to his sister as "My case of 'Jarndyce & Jarndyce.' "[45]

It does not seem necessary to speak here in any detail of Dickens's second Boston visit, for this has been adequately covered by others elsewhere. As Longfellow wrote to Forster:

> It is a great pleasure to see Dickens again after so many years, with the same sweetness and flavor as of old, and only greater ripeness. The enthusiasm for him and for his Readings is immense. One can hardly take in the whole truth about it, and feel the universality of his fame. The Readings will be as triumphant a success here as in England. Every ticket is sold for the whole course, and the public clamours for more.[46]

Yet he complains, more than once, that Boston audiences are cold:

> For the last two weeks Boston has been, not Galvanized but Dickenized into great activity, very pleasant to behold. The Readings, or rather Actings, have been immensely successful, according to our standard of success; but Boston audiences are proverbially cold. The Gulf Stream itself would hardly raise their temperature a degree.[47]

Dickens was too ill to attend Longfellow's birthday dinner on February 27, 1868, following his reading of the *Carol* and "Boots at the Holly Tree Inn," but he sent him one of the most charming

[45] MS: Samuel Longfellow, Letter to Anne Longfellow Pierce, Nov. 27, 1856.

[46] MS: HWL, Letter to John Forster, Nov. 23, 1867.

[47] MS: HWL, Letter to Charles Sumner, Dec. 8, 1867.

letters of affectionate greeting that any man ever wrote or received.[48] On the twenty-ninth, however, Longfellow attended the "grand banquet" which Dickens gave at the Parker House, in honor of the Boston publisher, James T. Fields. Longfellow pasted into his journal the beautiful colored place card and the bill of fare, printed inside a sheet of what seems to be Dickens's own letter paper, with the engraved monogram "CD" on the first page. On March 4 Longfellow himself had Dickens to dinner at the Craigie House; perhaps this was the time when the novelist, seeing a set of his own books on the shelves, exclaimed, "Ah, I see you read the good authors."[49]

Like the first Boston meeting between Longfellow and Dickens, the second quickly found a successor in England. In July (4–6), 1868, Dickens entertained Longfellow, his three daughters, and his brother-in-law, Thomas Gold Appleton, at Gad's Hill. This was the last time Longfellow and Dickens met.

According to a rather strange passage in Mrs. James T. Fields's journals, this meeting was not a great success:

> When Mr. L. talks so much and so pleasantly, I am curiously reminded of Dickens's saying to Forster, who lamented that he did not see Longfellow upon his return to London, "It was not a great loss this time, Forster; he had not a word to say for himself —he was the most embarrassing man in all England!" It is a difference of temperament which will never let those two men come together. They have no handle by which to take hold of each other. Longfellow told a gentleman at his table when J. was

[48] Cf. *The Letters of Charles Dickens* (Bloomsbury, The Nonesuch Press, 1938), III, 626.

[49] MS: HWL, Letter to Elizabeth Stuart Phelps, Mar. 7, 1879 (Courtesy, Boston Public Library).

present that Dickens saved himself for his books, there was nothing to be learned in private—he never talked!![50]

This may be true, though I have found no indication of it elsewhere. As early as 1843, however, Longfellow seems to have felt that both Dickens and Forster—"both good fellows in the main"—were "living in a strong hallucination about this country."[51] More interesting than any of this, however, are the comments which Longfellow makes on Dickens's domestic tragedy, on his death, and on Forster's biography of him.

When, in the spring of 1858, the news came that Dickens and his wife had separated, Longfellow was saddened, not only by the fact but by the gossip that came with it:

> What a sad affair is this of Dickens. Immensely exaggerated no doubt; but sad enough at best. How discouraging it is, and disgusting, to see how eagerly and recklessly a fair reputation is dragged through the mire of the streets.[52]

Just what had he heard? And how much of it did he believe? Mrs. Longfellow writes with similar ambiguousness to her sister Mary, in England:

> How sad is all this gossip about Dickens. I cannot believe the most of it, but it is a pity, since people will invent reasons, he cannot give the plain story of the trouble.[53]

Whatever the answer to these questions may be, the Longfellows

[50] May 24, 1870. Cf. M. A. DeWolfe Howe, ed., *Memories of a Hostess* ... (The Atlantic Monthly Press, 1922), 160.
[51] MS: HWL, Letter (in FEAL's hand) to Thomas G. Appleton, July 29, 1843.
[52] MS: HWL, Letter to Charles Sumner, June 3, 1858.
[53] MS: FEAL, Letter to Mary Mackintosh, June 22, 1858.

had no share in spreading the scandal, for even after Dickens had died, Longfellow spent half an hour with Fields at the print shop, urging him "to suppress certain things in his account of Dickens in the 'Whispering Gallery.' "[54]

This was in 1871, by which time he had adjusted himself to the shock of Dickens's death. When the news came, he wrote Forster:

> The terrible news from England fills us all with inexpressible grief. Dickens was so full of life, that it did not seem possible he could die, and yet he has gone before us, and we are the mourners. I know what this loss will be to you, and cannot speak of it. I will not try to speak of it.
>
> I hope his book is finished. It is certainly one of his most beautiful works, if not the most beautiful of all. It would be too sad to think the pen had fallen from his hand, and left it incomplete.
>
> I never knew an author's death cause such general mourning. It is no exaggeration to say that this whole country is stricken with grief. You can judge what it is, from what you see and hear around you in England.[55]

A week later, he writes his brother Alexander, "Dickens is seldom out of my thoughts. He is a great loss to the world."[56]

When Forster's *Life* of Dickens was published, the revelation of the novelist's driving restlessness contained in it overwhelmed Longfellow and oppressed him with melancholy thoughts. Writing to Charles Kent in 1878, he recalled his visit to Gad's Hill:

> How suddenly Dickens vanished from our sight! And yet I was not much surprised; for when he was last here he seemed

[54] MS: HWL, Journal, Aug. 30, 1871.
[55] MS: HWL, Letter to John Forster, June 12, 1870.
[56] MS: HWL, Letter to Alexander W. Longfellow, June 19, 1870.

87

very restless, as if driven by fate;—*fato profugus.* Whenever you meet Miss Hogarth, or any of the family, I beg you to remind them of me, and to say how gratefully I remember their hospitality.[57]

Five years before that he had already written Forster himself:

Charles Norton has arrived and has brought me your letter which touches me by its kindness. But I am grieved to hear that you have been so ill and suffering. Are you not overworked? To write the life of a dear friend—just gone, must be a task almost too painful.

How fearlessly and well you have done yours I need not say. I have read the two volumes with deepest interest and sympathy. You give an exact portrait of Dickens; and have had the courage not to conceal some things, that others might have hidden, but which make the likeness true and lifelike.

How sad it is to think that of all the group that used to meet in the happy days of Devonshire Terrace, so few remain! We will not think of it, or, at all events, not speak of it now.

I can well imagine without your saying it, how bitter this last volume will be to you. If Dickens had been dead a hundred years the task would be easier. But your skill will carry you through triumphantly.[58]

When the third volume came in 1874, he added:

Accept my warmest thanks for the third volume of your "life of Dickens." I have read it with intense interest. I congratulate you on the completion of your difficult and delicate task. It is an admir-

[57] MS: HWL, Letter to Charles Kent, Apr. 20, 1878 (Courtesy, The Estelle Doheny Collection of the Edward Laurence Doheny Memorial Library, St. John's Seminary, Camarillo, California).

[58] MS: HWL, Letter to John Forster, June 18, 1873.

able specimen of Biography; for if the object of biography is to present a man as he lived and moved and had his being here on earth, you have done it admirably.[59]

The final item is added in a letter to Longfellow's sister-in-law, Mary Mackintosh, in London, February 6, 1876:

I am sorry to read in the papers of the death of my old friend John Forster, in your neighborhood. He is the last of the Dickens circle. It has all vanished, like an exhalation![60]

And so the whole Round Table was dissolved.

IV

To these personal items I should like to add just one reflection: Dickens is the only novelist who can be suspected of having exercised an influence upon Longfellow's own style. There is a good deal in his novel *Kavanagh* (1849) which is quite in the spirit of Dickens whimsy: the description of Lucy and the baby at the beginning of Chapter II; the dismal clock in Chapter VIII— "gasping and catching its breath at times, and striking the hour with a violent, determined blow, reminding one of Jael driving the nail into the head of Sisera"; the poet H. Adolphus Hawkins, whose "shiny hair went off to the left in a superb sweep, like the curve of a banister"; and the ardent lover who sends his inamorata "letters written with his own blood—going barefooted into the brook to be bitten by leeches, and thus using his feet as inkstands." Quite like Dickens's animism, too, is the behavior of the little town at the beginning of "The Bell of Atri" (*Tales of a Wayside Inn*):

[59] MS: HWL, Letter to John Forster, Feb. 22, 1874.
[60] MS: HWL, Letter to Mary Mackintosh, Feb. 6, 1876.

One of those little places that have run
Half up the hill, beneath a blazing sun,
And then sat down to rest, as if to say,
"I climb no farther upward, come what may."

The same note sounds occasionally in the journals. When he received the first proofs of *Evangeline* in the cheap edition of his poems, Longfellow could not help wishing that a wider measure might have been used:

It certainly would be a relief to the hexameters to let them stretch their legs a little more at their ease; still for the sake of uniformity I believe they must sit a while longer with their knees bent under them like travellers in a stage-coach.[61]

In December, 1855, he entertained Thackeray, Ole Bull, and others at supper. Two guests failed to arrive. "We had," he says, "music on the Cremona, and then a *petit souper*, with two vacant places and plates looking on with hollow, hungry eyes."[62]

Once, too, in *Martin Chuzzlewit*, Dickens borrowed a figure from Longfellow—or so at least Longfellow thought he did. In the Preface to *Ballads and Other Poems* (1841), the American wrote:

In the church-yard are a few flowers, and much green grass; and daily the shadow of the church spire, with its long tapering finger, counts the tombs, representing a dial-plate of human life, on which the hours and minutes are the graves of men.

In Chapter V of his novel Dickens says:

In this way they went on, and on, and on—in the language of

[61] MS: HWL, Journal, Jan. 17, 1849.
[62] Samuel Longfellow, *Life*, II, 270.

the story-books—until at last the village lights appeared before them, and the church spire cast a long reflection on the grave-yard grass; as if it were a dial (alas, the truest in the world!) marking whatever light shone out of Heaven, the flight of days and weeks and year, by some new shadow on that solemn ground.

Longfellow put in his claim promptly in a letter to Forster, but he seems greatly pleased:

The figure of speech about the shadow of the church spire moving round the church-yard, as on a vast dial-plate, I claim as my own: See Preface to Ballads, p. xi—a very good figure notwithstanding.[63]

Whatever reservations may have been made upon either side, there is no room for doubt that for Henry Wadsworth Longfellow, Charles Dickens was the most important of all novelists.

[63] MS: HWL, Letter to John Forster, Feb. 28, 1843.

Dickens and Charles Fechter

DICKENS WAS ONE OF THE GREATEST theater "fans" on record, but there was no actor for whom he expressed greater enthusiasm than Charles Fechter, especially in the character of Hamlet. When Fechter was ready to visit America, Dickens actually beat the drums for him by publishing a laudatory article in *The Atlantic Monthly*.

For this he has been much criticized both by those who could not share his high opinion of the actor's talents and by those who held him in little regard as a man. Ralph Straus dismissed Fechter contemptuously as "an Anglo-French actor of little merit," and even J. W. T. Ley (*The Dickens Circle*, 1919) spoke of Dickens's interest in Fechter as an "obsession."[1]

There is an interesting item bearing upon Dickens's interest in Fechter in a book called *James T. Fields: Biographical Notes and Personal Sketches*, published in Boston in 1881 by Houghton, Mifflin and Company. Though no author is named on the title

[1] For commentary on Fechter's Hamlet, see William Winter, *Shakespeare on the Stage* (Moffat, Yard, 1911), 403–10. Admitting Fechter's technical skill and calling him a brilliant romantic actor in the Frédéric Lemaître tradition, Winter finds his conception of Hamlet basically wrong and declares that he could not read English blank verse. He admits, however, that Fechter was greatly admired by both Wilkie Collins and Kate Field.

page, the book is known to have been written by Fields's widow, Annie Fields.

James T. Fields, as all Dickensians know, was the Boston publisher who was instrumental in bringing Dickens to the United States for the phenomenal reading tour of 1868, and he and his wife were perhaps the most intimate of the novelist's American friends. Indeed, one often wonders whether, without their loving care of him during his trying illnesses, he might not have died on this side of the Atlantic.

There is considerable mention of Fechter in the Fields book, but perhaps the most interesting passage is this:

> Dickens possessed a strong influence over Fechter, and while he lived, seemed to keep him from sinking. He said, however, when Fechter decided to come to America, "He will doubtless make a great impression, but whether anything can prevent him from overturning his own fortunes remains to be seen. I shall do the best I can for him."

These words are obviously quoted from memory and can hardly be entirely accurate. Mrs. Fields was, however, a careful and capable woman, her husband was editor of the *Atlantic* at the time Dickens's article appeared in it, and she can hardly have mistaken the *tenor* of what Dickens meant to say. The words quoted seem, therefore, to throw considerable light on Dickens's attitude toward Fechter and, indeed, upon Dickens as a friend.

Of course this does not mean that Dickens was in any way insincere in what he had written about Fechter as an actor. We do not need the *Atlantic* article to prove that Dickens considered Fechter a fine actor; the letters alone prove that. And since none of us can now go to see the actor and study his performances, a study of Dickens's dramatic criticism in this aspect hardly seems in order.

What is interesting is that, in the light of Mrs. Fields's record, it no longer seems necessary—or even possible—to regard Dickens, in his relations with Fechter, as having been bewitched by a second-rate man. He admired Fechter as an actor, but he was not unaware that there were grave elements of weakness in his character, sources of danger which might well, and in spite of his gifts, lead him finally to make a wreck of his life. Envisaging this possibility, Dickens went to work to help Fechter by encouraging him toward the completest and most useful exercise of his talents that was possible for him. This was a wise and kindly action, and it causes the Fechter episode in Dickens's career to emerge in a new light. So far from being something to be ashamed of, it illustrates at once his brotherliness and his penetration, doing equal credit to his heart and to his head.

Dickens and Ellen Glasgow

ELLEN GLASGOW's INTEREST in the novels of Charles Dickens is well known. In her fine commentary upon her own most important fictions, she listed *David Copperfield* among the books for which she would "die upon the literary barricade."[1] Elsewhere, she goes so far as to say that she is not sure whether her lifelong inclination toward placing herself "on the side of the disinherited" was due, in the beginning, to her love for Dickens, or whether it was this tendency in her own temperament which drew her to him.[2] But neither in anything that she wrote about herself nor in anything that others have written about her have I ever found any reference to the obvious indebtedness of the first section (Chapters I–IV) of her eighth novel, *The Romance of a Plain Man* (1909), to the magnificent opening chapters of *Great Expectations*.

The most obvious resemblance between the two works is shown in the child Sally's objection to the "common boy," Ben Starr, and the "commonplace" world which he inhabits. In *Great Expectations*, "common" is the very key word of Estella's association with Pip. In both novels, the boy, who has been strongly taken with the attractive girl, is hurt and determines to lift himself out

[1] Ellen Glasgow, *A Certain Measure* (Harcourt, Brace, 1943), 190.
[2] Ellen Glasgow, "What I Believe," *Nation*, Vol. CXXXVI (1933), 404–406.

of his class. It is true that Sally is a much pleasanter girl than Estella and has much less desire to wound: later she calls Benjy "a dear little fellow, with such pretty blue eyes." But an Estella-like pertness of manner clings to her all through her childhood.

Though Ben Starr's poor home is in the city, and not out upon the marshes as Pip's was, Ellen Glasgow surrounded it with "atmosphere"—in which heavy, rainy weather is the principal ingredient—which is very similar to the atmosphere that had been created by Dickens. There is a church hard by, and Benjy is threatened with a whipping if he goes to the churchyard. Benjy's father is a stonecutter; Pip was much given to pondering the inscriptions on the gravestones. Sally and her mother appear as fugitives in the first chapter of *The Romance of a Plain Man*, and Ben's father kindly covers their tracks, as Pip tried to protect his convict in *Great Expectations*. (Ben's sight of a "big black figure splashing recklessly through the heavy puddles under the faint yellowish glimmer of the street lamp at the corner" recalls Pip's fascinated scrutiny of the progress of the convict across the marshes.)

In general, Ben's mother corresponds to Pip's sister, Mrs. Gargery, and his father to Joe. Mrs. Starr is, to be sure, no such ogre as Mrs. Gargery. Mrs. Gargery would certainly not have allowed Pip to bring home a dog; neither would she have brought the dog inside, to comfort it, on its first night in its new home, as Mrs. Starr does, after having first made Ben thoroughly miserable, up to his bedtime, by her complaints about its howling. But she is clearly more stern than her husband, who is Ben's comforter, as Joe comforted Pip, and of whom the boy asks endless questions, much in the Pip manner. Any Dickensian child would have been fascinated, as Ben is, by his mother's grotesque shadow upon the wall, and Mrs. Starr's complaint in Chapter II of the wrong she suffers in being compelled to wear her mourning in the house is very close to Mrs. Gargery's lament that she has never had her apron off since Pip was born.

Pip never meets Estella until he goes to Miss Havisham's house to "play"; Ben Starr first encounters Sally in his own house, when she and her mother take (so far as the child is concerned) disdainful refuge there. But he desires thereafter to go to the big house where the little girl lives—"an' it's got a big garden—as big as that!" There is no Miss Havisham in the house, but there is an eccentric grandmother, of grotesque appearance and tyrannical ways. When Ben finally gets in,

> There was a strange musty smell about the house—a smell that brings to me now, when I find it in old and unlighted buildings, the memory of the high ceiling, the shining floor over which I moved so cautiously, and the long melancholy rows of moth-eaten stags' heads upon the wall.

While as for the old woman herself,

> She was so little and thin and wrinkled that it was a mystery to me, as I looked at her, how she managed to express so much authority through so small a medium. The chair in which she sat seemed almost to swallow her in its high arms of faded green leather; and out of her wide, gathered skirt of brocade, her body rose very erect, like one of my mother's blackheaded bonnet pins out of her draped pincushion. On her head there was a cap of lace trimmed gayly with purple ribbons, and beneath this festive adornment, a fringe of false curls, still brown and lustrous, lent a ghastly coquetry to her mummied features.

Not Miss Havisham, certainly, and not Miss Havisham's house, but perhaps a not unworthy descendant of both.

It is notable, too, that the "feeling" of this whole first section of *The Romance of a Plain Man* is Dickensian. The very title of the first chapter—"In Which I Appear with Few Pretensions"—has a Dickensian ring. Ben's brother, President, has been eccentrically named, and the name arrived at by a process of reasoning which Dickens would surely have relished. The elder Starr's "I'm not an eater, mum," when Sally's mother, in her need, fears that she is drawing him away from his dinner, is worthy of any Dickens character, and the whole account of the funeral to which Mrs. Starr drags her boy, to say nothing of his behavior there, is in the Dickens manner.

I must make it very clear that I am not reproaching Ellen Glasgow for her borrowings from *Great Expectations*. She borrowed and she recharactered. She showed her sensitiveness to fine quality in fiction by responding so enthusiastically as she did to what is perhaps the most brilliant sequence of chapters in all Dickens, and she showed her skill as a novelist by herself creating in a similar mood in her own milieu. While not equal to its inspiration, the result was, in my judgment, the most delightful series of scenes she had so far created.

Dickens and Katherine Mansfield

"Yes—doesn't Charley D. make our little men smaller than
ever—and such *pencil sharpeners*—"

K.M., August 22nd, 1918

I

IT WAS WHILE READING the unfinished "Married Man's Story,"
included in the volume known as *The Doves' Nest and Other
Stories,* that I first became conscious of a certain Dickensian flavor
in the writing of Katherine Mansfield. The story is written in the
first person, and the earliest passage to catch my eye was that in
which the narrator describes his attitude towards his own baby:

> A queer thing is I can't connect him with my wife and myself;
> I've never accepted him as ours. Each time when I come into the
> hall and see the perambulator, I catch myself thinking: "H'm,
> someone has brought a baby."

A little further on, we have this fancy of the narrator's
childhood:

> But really to explain what happened then I should have to go
> back and back, I should have to dwindle until my two hands
> clutched the banisters, the stair-rail was higher than my head, and
> I peered through to watch my father padding softly up and down.
> There were coloured windows on the landings. As he came up,
> first his bald head was scarlet; then it was yellow. How frightened
> I was! And when they put me to bed, it was to dream that we
> were living inside one of my father's big coloured bottles. For he
> was a chemist.

Best of all, however, are two descriptions of the narrator's father as seen through his own childish eyes. The first relates to no particular occasion. The second is a snapshot of the father at the funeral of his wife, whom their child believes him to have murdered:

> Perfectly bald, polished head, shaped like a thin egg, creased, creamy cheeks, little bags under his eyes, large pale ears like handles.

> That tall hat so gleaming black and round was like a cork covered with black sealing-wax, and the rest of my father was awfully like a bottle, with his face for the label—*Deadly Poison.* . . . And Deadly Poison, or old D.P., was my private name for him from that day.

The emphasis on ridiculous and ludicrous detail, the flair for eccentric physical characteristics, the sharp eye for vivid contrasts, the absurd, unexpected—yet true—psychological reaction, and the farfetched—at the same time amusing and suggestive—comparison —all this, presented as it appears here, seems to me distinctly Dickensian.

I find similar touches in other stories. In "Mr. and Mrs. Williams," in the same volume, we read: "As a matter of fact it was Mrs. Williams' Aunt Aggie's happy release which had made their scheme possible. Happy release it was! After fifteen years in a wheel-chair . . . she had, to use the nurse's expression, 'just glided away at the last.' Glided away . . . it sounded as though Aunt Aggie had taken the wheel chair with her. One saw her, in her absurd purple velvet, steering carefully among the stars and whimpering faintly, as was her terrestrial wont, when the wheel jolted over a particularly large one." In the title story of this volume, Prodger complains that it is very difficult to live in a hotel where you cannot get a hot plate by ringing for it. "Mother, though outwardly all sympathy, found this a little bewildering. She had a momentary vision of Mr. Prodger ringing for hot plates to be brought to him at all hours. Such strange things to want in any numbers." In "The Doll's House," Katherine Mansfield manifests very strikingly Dickens's ability effectively to "tag" a character through the vivid description of some characteristic action. Here little Else Kelvey goes through life "holding on to Lil, with a piece of Lil's skirt screwed up in her hand." The eighth section of "At the Bay" (in *The Garden Party*) is quite in the Dickens tradition, and some of it is as funny as *The Pickwick Papers*, but unfortunately it is too long to quote here.

Katherine Mansfield, as everybody knows, was a very "modern" writer. She was a friend of D. H. Lawrence. She had a decided affinity with Chekhov. It was for just such passages as I have here quoted that her admirers were praising her at the time I first noticed them. Yet they decidedly recalled the "mid-Victorian" Dickens. I promised myself that someday I would write a book called "Dickens Among the Moderns," in which I should collect all the astonishingly "new" devices, all the brave, fresh perceptions of the "modern" writers, all the tricks and quips that our erudite modern critics have hailed as something new under the sun. Then I would find a parallel for each of them in the "mid-Victorian" Dickens and thus demonstrate that everything the moderns have done that is worth doing was done by him long ago.

The book has never been written, and probably never will be. There is less need for it now than there was then. For whatever else about him may still be obscure, Dickens's astonishing technical forwardness is now much better understood than it was then.

II

The appearance, in 1927, of Katherine Mansfield's *Journal*, followed by the publication of two large volumes of *Letters*, shed considerable light on the possible influence of Dickens upon her, and thus made it possible for me to check up, in a measure, upon my previous impressions.

It appears that from 1915 on, Katherine Mansfield was reading Dickens a good deal, though there are many more references to him in the first volume of the *Letters* than in the second. On December 19, 1915, she writes her husband from the south of France:

> Dear, *do* send me summat to read when you can. I am still confined to Shakespeare and the *Times*. I don't know what to ask for. I'd like a 1/– Dickens that I haven't read—or one I don't remember—but which is it? Oh, I'd like to read *Oliver Twist* again, for one.

On January 16, 1918, she writes: "Please try and send me a book, a Dickens would do. I have read *Barnaby Rudge* twice. What about *Our Mutual Friend*? Is that good? I've never read it." A few days later, on February 1, she asks for *Nicholas Nickleby*, and on February 20, she writes: "Can I have another Dickens some time?—*Bleak House* or *Edwin Drood*?"

I wish we had her comments on all these books. What we do have is this on *Our Mutual Friend* (January 8, 1918):

> Have you read *Our Mutual Friend*? Some of it is really *damned good*. The satire in it is first chop—all the Veneering business *par example* could not be better. I'd never read it before and I'm enjoying it immensely. Ma Wilfer is after my own heart.

I have a huge capacity for seeing "funny" people, you know, and Dickens does fill it at all times quite amazingly.

But her most enthusiastic praise is reserved for *David Copperfield*, which she had probably read before leaving England in search of the health she never regained. Writing to her friend, Lady Ottoline Morrell, August 22, 1918, she says: *"Isn't* David Copperfield adorable? I like even the Dora part, and that friend of Dora's—Julia—somebody, who was 'blighted.' She is such a joy to me."

Besides these, there are several incidental references which go to show that Dickens was often in the background of Katherine Mansfield's mind. Once she refers to "the Micawber family starting off for Australia" (August 1, 1917). Again, she remarks: "My lovely gay shawl lies upon a chair and I gaze at it feeling rather like David Copperfield's Dora, and wondering when I shall wear it again" (January 18, 1918). And still again, paying her compliments to the intelligentsia, she writes: "They make one feel like that poor foreigner arraigned before Mr. Podsnap on the hearthrug in *Our Mutual Friend"* (August 24, 1922).

It is good to know that once during her sad illness, in December, 1917, Dickens helped Katherine Mansfield to ward off some unwelcome coddling:

> Mrs. N. came in last night and wanted to whisk me off to her house for a few days. Oh, what a dread prospeck! The amount of whisking that people want to do with me and a-wrapping of me up in bundils is quite terrifying. I said I was being superbly looked after by old Mrs. Harris, who was a very good cook. Oh! What fun! Do you know who I meant? Sairey Gamp's friend. I laughed so much inside that I thought she would hear the laughs running

up and down in me. Even to write it makes me laugh again, and Ribni [her Japanese doll] stuffed the ends of his necktie in his mouth, stood on his head and waved his feet when I told him.

It is interesting also to note that Katherine Mansfield, besides appreciating Dickens, appreciated Forster's *Life*.

There is a book which we must positively not be another week without. It is Forster's *Life of Dickens*. How is it that people refer to this and have many a time and oft talked of it to me and yet— as though it was a very good Life, a very good Life indeed, about as good as you could get and immensely well worth reading. But so dispassionately—so as a matter of course. Merciful Heavens! It's one of the most absolutely fascinating books I have ever set eyes on. I found to-day Vol. III. in the book shelves. Whether the other two are here or not I don't know, but I do most solemnly assure you it is so great that it were worth while building a house in the country and putting in fireplaces, chairs and a table, curtains, hot wine and you and me and Richard and whoever else we "fancy" exprès for reading this. It's *ravishing*. What will you do when you come to the description of how his little boy, aged four, plays the part of hero in a helmet and sword at their theatricals and having previously made the dragon drunk on sherry stabs him dead, which he does in such a manner that Thackeray falls off his chair, laughing, and rolls on the floor. No, that's nothing. Read of his landlord, *M. Beaufort*, read of his home in Boulogne.

Now I am exaggerating. Since I wrote all that I finished the book. It's not GREAT, of course, it's not; it's fascinating and it's a bit terrible as a lesson. I never knew what killed Dickens. It was money. He couldn't, as he grew older, resist money; he became a miser and disguised it under a laughing exterior. Money and applause—he died for both. How fearful that is! But still we must have the book. We must have his complete works . . . (February, 1920).

III

But the most interesting part of our story is yet to be told. So far, Dickens would hardly seem to have furnished anything more than recreation for Katherine Mansfield. Indeed she writes, February 3, 1918: "That is why I asked for another Dickens; if I read him in bed he diverts my mind. My work excites me so tremendously that I almost feel *insane* at night, and I have been at it with hardly a break all day." But two days before she had remarked: "I am not reading Dickens *idly*." It seems to me she was right about this, but in order to show how, I must go rather far afield.

Many years ago, in *My Father As I Recall Him*, Mamie Dickens told a very interesting story about what happened one morning while she watched her father at work:

> I was lying on the sofa endeavoring to keep perfectly quiet, while my father wrote busily and rapidly at his desk, when he suddenly jumped from his chair and rushed to a mirror which hung near and in which I could see the reflection of some extra-ordinary facial contortions which he was making. He returned rapidly to his desk, wrote furiously for a few moments, and then went again to the mirror. The facial pantomime was resumed, and then turning towards, but evidently not seeing me, he began talking in a low voice. Ceasing this soon, however, he returned once more to his desk, where he remained silently writing until luncheon time.

It would have been easy to dismiss this performance as simply manifesting the eccentricity of genius, but Miss Dickens's own conviction was that her father had actually thrown himself into the character he was creating. This interpretation is supported by at least two other references. In a letter of Dickens to Forster, written while he was working on *Barnaby Rudge*, Dickens wrote: "I have just burst into Newgate, and am going in the next number to tear the prisoners out by the hair of their heads." Again, in the Preface to *A Tale of Two Cities*, he remarks that when he first conceived the idea of the story, he immediately became anxious to embody it in his own person. "Throughout its execution, it has had complete possession of me; I have so far verified what is done and suffered in those pages, as that I have certainly done and suffered it all myself."

Katherine Mansfield sensed this, as it were, experiencial quality in Dickens:

> There are moments when Dickens is possessed by this power of writing; he is carried away. That is bliss. It certainly is not shared by writers to-day. The death of Merdle: dawn falling upon the edge of night. One realises exactly the mood of the writer and how he wrote, as it were, for himself, but it was not his will. He *was* the falling dawn, and he *was* the physician going to Bar (*Journal*, February 29, 1920).

We may say then, I believe, that Katherine Mansfield discerned a certain affinity between this aspect of Dickens and her own artistic experience. Four passages from the letters are apropos here:

> When I write about ducks I swear that I am a white duck with a round eye, floating on a pond fringed with yellow-blobs and taking an occasional dart at the other duck with the round eye, which floats upside down beneath me. . . . In fact the whole process of becoming the duck (what Lawrence would perhaps call this consummation with the duck or the apple!) is so thrilling that I can hardly breathe, only to think about it. For although that is as far as most people can get, it is really only the "prelude." There follows the moment when you are *more* duck, *more* apple, or

more Natasha than any of these objects could ever possibly be, and so you *create* them anew (October 11, 1917).

In my dream I saw a supper-table with the eyes of *five*. It was awfully queer—especially a plate of half-melted ice-cream . . . (February 10–11, 1918).

What a QUEER business writing is! I don't know. I don't believe other people are ever as foolishly excited as I am while I'm working. How could they be? Writers would have to live in trees. I've *been* this man, *been* this woman. I've stood for hours on the Auckland Wharf. I've been out in the stream waiting to be berthed— I've been a seagull hovering at the stern and a hotel porter whistling through his teeth. It isn't as though one sits and watches the spectacle. That would be thrilling enough, God knows. But one is the spectacle for the time (November 3, 1920).

In his book, *The Actor in Dickens*, J. B. Van Amerongen quotes the passage from *My Father As I Recall Him* that I have given here, and uses it to show that Dickens created his characters first as an actor. Therefore, he contends brilliantly and convincingly, it is very inadequate to dismiss the influence of the theater on Dickens with a few superior remarks about his melodrama and his sensationalism. The theater was inwrought with the very fiber of Dickens's art, the highest elements in it as well as the lowest. Had it not been for the theater, Dickens's novels as we now know them could never have been. He created his characters as an actor. He gave himself to his art, and put his people together out of his own life.

IV

This essay is not an exercise in source-hunting. I have not proved nor sought to prove that Katherine Mansfield had Dickens in mind when she wrote the stories alluded to in my first section. That would not interest me very much, one way or the other. What I am much more interested in is the eager response of the one artist to the other, and this seems to me an honor to them both. It is evident from the passages already cited that Katherine Mansfield's real experience with Dickens came in her last years, though doubtless she had read some of his novels earlier. If it cannot be pretended that he influenced her as Chekhov did, or that she read him with the rapture with which she read Shakespeare or Dostoevski, still it is significant that she is utterly free from the snobbish, superior attitude that so many of these latter-day exclusive "geniuses" have manifested. The most important consideration that emerges is, however, the striking resemblance between what I have called the dramatic or the experiencial approach in both of them.

This is superbly theatrical. That is, it is exactly the opposite of what most people mean when they say theatrical; it is genuine and vital and unashamed. We have seen that Katherine Mansfield appreciated this in Dickens; that she took it as marking the significant difference between Dickens and her own contemporaries, and that she strove to achieve the same thing for herself. Under the circumstances, she can hardly have been wholly unaware that she was, in her own way, following in his footsteps.

Dickens and the Marxians

ONCE THERE WAS A SHAKESPEAREAN CRITIC named Denton J. Snider. He knew his Shakespeare well, but he had certain gods of his idolatry which (like King Charles's head) insisted on thrusting themselves into everything he wrote. There was the sanctity of the family. There was the sanctity of the state. There was poetic justice. Now if a Shakespearean critic believes in poetic justice it becomes necessary for him to prove that everybody who suffers or dies in Shakespeare's plays is quite as guilty as he is unfortunate. Snider had a dreadful time of it when he came to such innocents as Desdemona and Romeo and Juliet, but he rose to the occasion nobly. Desdemona deserved to die because she lied to Othello about the handkerchief. As for Romeo and Juliet, he admitted that their love for each other was genuine and pure. But it was selfish, limited. They loved each other. They ought to have been devoted to the family as an institution.

The patent absurdity of such judgments illustrates the dangers which beset the doctrinaire mind in criticism. And since the Marxian and the Freudian are, among all modern men, the least free and the most enslaved to dogma, it is hardly surprising that when they turn to literary criticism they encounter a pitfall per page and never miss falling into a single one.

Mr. Jackson's study of Dickens[1] is perhaps not quite so bad as it might have been. Though there are some curious errors of fact, one may still say in general that he knows the novels well. Certainly he loves them passionately. When he permits himself to forget his thesis, he is nearly always excellent. At such moments he lays aside the blinders which Karl Marx has fastened upon him and tells us what he sees, what is there, not what he would like to think is there. And it should be accounted unto him for righteousness that when Dickens disappoints him, he never loses his temper. This point of view is very refreshing to one who has been reading, let us say, Van Wyck Brooks or Edgar Lee Masters on Mark Twain.

Mr. Jackson does not attempt to show that Dickens was a Communist. Ah, no! but he would have been if only Mr. Jackson or somebody like him could have made him see the light. (Lyman Beecher thought that perhaps he might have converted Byron.) Dickens's "tragedy" was that while he lost "the old optimist faith in bourgeois society," he never acquired that "faith in the proletariat and its revolutionary mission" which gives meaning to Mr. Jackson's life. Of men born of women none was greater than he but the least is greater in the kingdom of Marx.

It would be difficult to get the thing more completely wrong. Of course Dickens sympathized with the poor, no man more so. Of course he hated oppression. Besides being a great novelist, he was a great social reformer. But he approached these problems, as he approached life itself, emotionally, intuitively, not intellectually or, above all, schematically. Never in a thousand years could he

[1] T. A. Jackson, *Charles Dickens, The Progress of a Radical* (International Publishers, 1938).

have delivered himself over to a system. He hated system, hated government; he was an individualist to the core. His was exactly the opposite kind of mind to Mr. Jackson's—a much commoner kind among Anglo-Saxons incidentally. His rebellion was directed against specific abuses; he addressed his pleas to the heart and conscience of the individual. He never sought to escape the shortcomings of one system by setting up another. Had he been a true revolutionary, anarchism might have tempted him, communism never.

Dickens deals with revolution in two books. With *Barnaby Rudge* even Mr. Jackson can do nothing. Of *A Tale of Two Cities* he makes the amazing statement that it "showed a complete and whole-hearted sympathy with the revolutionaries." To justify this view, he first turns the book around: "the real drama is an implicit drama, which the foreground action-drama serves only to symbolize."

This is characteristic of Mr. Jackson's whole method. He is very successful in telling us what he can read into Dickens's novels. He rarely succeeds in showing that what he reads is what Dickens wrote. Indeed, he is more or less committed to the thesis that Dickens didn't know what he was writing but that Jackson does. *Little Dorrit*, for example, is "an allegory of whose true purport its author was only partly conscious."

Dickens did, of course, use *A Tale of Two Cities* to teach England the danger of revolution. He tells us that specifically. Outrage begets outrage is what he is saying. Love begets love. Permit such conditions to exist as existed in France toward the end of the eighteenth century, and you will get what France got. Himself he approves neither the abuses themselves nor the outrages that resulted from them.

Mr. Jackson has a dreadful time when he comes to Dickens's religion. In their simple, emotional, quite undoctrinal way, his novels are, as William Lyon Phelps once remarked, virtually a commentary on the Four Gospels. At one point Mr. Jackson suggests that the religious element may have been included as a concession to popular taste, or (*mirabile dictu!*) may have been added by John Forster. Like George Henry Lewes, Dickens loved the theater, and he appreciated George Eliot's gifts as a novelist; does it not then follow that, like the two Georges, he must have inclined toward unbelief? But in spite of all such nonsense, in the last analysis Mr. Jackson cannot do much more about Dickens's religion than fall back on head-shaking over his "inconsistency and vacillation." "He is not, it must be conceded, openly anti-religious." Mr. Jackson, it must be conceded, is not much of a critic. But as a humorist he ranks high.

The follower of Marx makes much of Dickens's many criticisms of religious persons and practices. What he never even begins to understand is that Dickens condemns these things because they are not Christian enough. He tests them by the spirit of Jesus Christ and finds them wanting. He can find no warrant for them in the New Testament. Some of Mr. Jackson's own quotations show this. He should be more careful about his quotations.

Absurdity could hardly go further than this, yet it does. Mr. Jackson has a new explanation of the reason why Mr. and Mrs. Dickens separated, and it is so fantastic that it makes the lucubrations of the wildest anti-Ternanites look sensible: "The facts are only accounted for if we conclude that the really fundamental incompatability between Dickens and his wife lay in the complete antithesis of their convictions about contemporary society as a whole."

No comment of mine could add anything to that. Not even Mr. Jackson could add anything to that. Mercifully I ring down the curtain.

Edmund Wilson on Dickens

IN AN ESSAY ON PHILOCTETES which he prints last in his book[1] for
no apparent reason except that it had better be read first, Mr.
Wilson explains his characteristically cryptic title. Philoctetes had
a bow which made him invincible, but Philoctetes also had a wound
which stubbornly refused to heal; when the Greeks had need of
him before Troy they found it impossible to get the bow without
accepting the wound.

What does all this mean for literature in general and for the
six writers studied specifically in *The Wound and the Bow?* Mr.
Wilson does not actually say that the creator creates because he has
suffered a psychic wound. He contents himself by finding "a
general and fundamental idea" in the Philoctetes story—"the conception of superior strength as inseparable from disability." In
another connection he refers to "the idea that genius and disease,
like strength and mutilation, may be inextricably bound up
together."

This thesis, if thesis it be, does not appear in the paper on
James Joyce, which is merely a guide to *Finnegans Wake*, nor does
it importantly affect the sensitive study of Ernest Hemingway.
There is some suggestion of it in the picture of Casanova as a poten-

---

[1]Edmund Wilson, *The Wound and the Bow: Seven Studies in Literature*
(Houghton Mifflin, 1941).

tially great man who was never able quite to emerge "from some heritage of moral squalor." But when we come to Dickens, Kipling, and Edith Wharton, there is another tale to tell. Mrs. Wharton's husband was unbalanced—even a psychic wound at second hand is better, it seems, than none at all; Kipling, like Conrad's Flora de Barral, suffered a brutally murdered childhood; virtually everything in the life and work of Dickens was determined by the unhappy experience in the blacking warehouse which he recorded as fiction in *David Copperfield*.

The parallel with Philoctetes cannot be made to go on all fours in connection with any one of these writers. Philoctetes had his bow before he acquired his wound, and he was never able to bend it against the walls of Troy until after his wound had been cured. ("Yet it is also decreed that he shall be cured when he shall have been able to forget his grievance and to devote his divine gifts to the service of his own people.") But Mrs. Wharton wrote her best novels during the years when her (or Edward Wharton's) wound bled; once she had been cured (in the form of a separation from him) and had settled down comfortably in France, she did little of significance (though, to be sure, Mr. Wilson adds casually that he has not read many of her later books). And neither Kipling's wound nor that of Dickens ever healed. Kipling was a case of arrested development; Dickens did "devote his divine gifts to the service of his own people," yet he made shipwreck of his personal life.

Essentially Mr. Wilson must stand or fall in this book with Kipling and Dickens. The Dickens study alone takes up more than one-third of his total space, and Dickens-plus-Kipling is nearly twice as long as all the rest put together. My primary concern here is with the Dickens.

115

Mr. Wilson has little respect for his predecessors in Dickensian criticism. He respects Gissing. He respects Bernard Shaw.
But Chesterton "is always melting away into that peculiar pseudo-
poetic booziness which verbalizes with large conceptions and
ignores the most obtrusive actualities"; Santayana, apparently, is
not even worth mentioning. This point of view seems rather
characteristic of Mr. Wilson; all who came before him were thieves
and robbers. His Kipling is "The Kipling That Nobody Read";
he comes gallantly to do "Justice to Edith Wharton"; he begins
his study of Casanova by assuring us that except for Havelock
Ellis's essay there is "nothing very serious" about him in English.

A critic who set up serious pretensions can hardly blame a
reviewer for taking him seriously. And a Dickensian critic who
calls his study of Dickens "The Two Scrooges" can hardly object
to a reader who looks first at his view of Scrooge. Here is what Mr.
Wilson says of that character, and the quotation is typical of his
whole essay:

> Shall we ask what Scrooge would be like if we were to follow him
> beyond the frame of the story? Unquestionably he would relapse
> when the merriment was over—if not while it was still going on—
> into moroseness, vindictiveness, suspicion. He would, that is to
> say, reveal himself as the victim of a manic-depressive cycle, and a
> very uncomfortable person.

I submit that this passage is as glaring an example of critical
irresponsibility as the reader is likely to find. If a critic finds the
conversion of Scrooge unconvincing, let him say so; he will find
many who agree with him. If he concludes that, therefore, the
Carol is worthless as literature, he is still entitled to his findings,
though now I, for one, will not agree with him. But we cannot

follow Scrooge "beyond the frame of the story," for the simple reason that beyond the frame of the story he does not exist. He is not a historical character; he is a character of fiction. To ignore this point or to obscure it is to confuse art with life and disqualify one-self as a critic of fiction altogether. And to take a character con-ceived in the tradition of popular melodrama and the Christmas pantomime (and completely accountable for in terms of that tradition) and attempt to interpret him in terms of a Freudian psychology which his creator not only did not accept but never heard of—this surely is to put oneself in a class with the unscholarly people who used to write essays on "The Girlhood of Shakespeare's Heroines" and speculate about what Goneril and Regan were doing when they were not on the stage.

Moreover, Mr. Wilson's handling of factual matters is quite as irresponsible as his criticism. This can best be illustrated in his treatment of Ellen Ternan.

Of course Mr. Wilson has a perfect right to believe that Ellen Ternan was Dickens's mistress if it seems to him that the evidence supports this view, or even that she bore him a child. He also has a perfect right to take Mrs. Dickens's part in her quarrel with her husband (if that is the word for it). But this is a very different thing from speaking of the novelist's alleged transgressions, as Mr. Wilson does, without giving the reader an inkling that there is any more doubt about them than there is about the fact that Dickens was born on February 7, 1812. It is different, too, from making such fantastic suggestions as that when Dickens wrote the story of the "cheap jack" Doctor Marigold, "who keeps an audience enter-tained with his patter [i.e., Dickens's readings] while his child is dying in his arms," he was writing autobiography, and that he liked to read the murder of Nancy because "the scene was perhaps a symbolical representation of his behavior in banishing his wife"! (Incidentally, *Oliver Twist* was published in 1838, just twenty years before Mr. and Mrs. Dickens separated.) Finally, I submit Mr. Wilson had no license for the method he uses to uncover Ellen Ternan's personality. We do not, he says, know what Ellen was like. He therefore assumes that the heroines of Dickens's last novels were studied from her; next he describes these heroines; finally he presents the result as a composite portrait of Ellen Ternan!

Mr. Wilson makes much of Dickens's nervous instability. The presence of this strain in him cannot be denied. All responsible critics have recognized the profoundly unsettling effect of both his squalid boyhood and his unhappy mismating. But before we conclude that Dickens must have sympathized with rebels and criminals because he wrote about crime, we ought at least to remember that (to go no farther back), Bulwer, Ainsworth, and others had established the Newgate novel before him. If Dickens was unbalanced because he loved terror tales, what is to be said of the whole Gothic school? Can we read psychological significances into his practical jokes without remembering that he is following in the Smollett tradition? Can we consider his *Tendenz-roman* intelligently without even a glance toward Holcroft and his contemporaries?[2]

[2] These backgrounds have now been studied by Keith Hollingsworth in *The Newgate Novel, 1830–1847* (Wayne State University Press, 1963); see, too, Philip Collins's excellent book, *Dickens and Crime* (Macmillan, 1962). It is amusing that Hollingsworth's knowledge in an area which Wilson gives no indication of having mastered has not prevented him from swallowing all the latter's nonsense about Dickens's "identification with murderers" (*The Newgate Novel*, 125). Collins furnishes adequate correctives at this point.

There has never been a time when Dickens's reputation as an artist stood higher than it stands today. The silly disparagement to which the twenties gave themselves is past; Mr. Wilson himself yields to nobody in his enthusiasm. But understanding does not seem to be keeping pace with appreciation. Mr. Wilson is well aware that T. A. Jackson spoiled what might otherwise have been an excellent book by putting on Marxian blinders before writing it; it seems strange that he should fail to perceive that Freud is to him what Marx was to Jackson.

It is a great pity that this should be the case, for it is clear that if Mr. Wilson had read Dickens with his eyes open, he might have produced the essay for which we have been waiting. A great deal has been made of his having "solved" the mystery of Edwin Drood. This is nonsense. He has ably summarized the studies of Howard Duffield and Aubrey Boyd, but his attempt to combine them, and to read Jasper full of autobiographical significance, quite misses fire. There are other things in his book that are really distinguished however: the study of Dickens's "symbols," for example, and Mr. Wilson's clear realization that Dickens underwent a consistent development as an artist.

It is important for much more than the study of Dickens that irresponsibility in criticism should be challenged. Dickens, after all, has no real need of protection. It is true that when Van Wyck Brooks went off the deep end over Mark Twain in 1920, he misled the "intelligentsia" for a whole decade. But DeVoto, Miss Brashear, and others led the way back to sanity; today we have recovered the real Mark Twain. The same thing will happen with Dickens. But it can happen only as writers learn how to handle evidence. The really disturbing thing about *The Wound and the*

Bow is not that it should have been written but that it should have found such eager acceptance among many people who ought to know better. Evidently it is not only in the political sphere that what Julien Benda called *le trahison des clercs* is to be repeated in our time.

A Tale of Two Cities[1]

A Tale of Two Cities was not the first novel about the French Revolution, but it set the tone for many of its successors. In England, both Bulwer-Lytton (*Zanoni*, 1842) and Anthony Trollope (*La Vendée*, 1850) had preceded Dickens in using the Revolutionary background; so, in France, had Dumas and Balzac. But none of these works has exercised an influence at all comparable to that of the story of Sydney Carton. Nor would many readers maintain that either *The Scarlet Pimpernel* of Baroness Orczy (1905) or Rafael Sabatini's *Scaramouche* (1921)—to name but two among the productions of later writers—is really in the same class.

It was one of the last of Dickens's novels, and it came out of a very troubled period in his life. The idea first came to the author in the summer of 1857, while he was acting, for charity, in his friend Wilkie Collins's play, *The Frozen Deep*. During the following restless winter, he found himself turning it over in his mind, haunted, at the same time, by "one strong possession of change impending over us that every day makes stronger." He pondered many titles, among them *One of These Days, The Doctor of Beauvais, Buried Alive* (which was destined to be saved, for use, in

[1] From the Introduction, by Edward Wagenknecht, to *A Tale of Two Cities*, by Charles Dickens. Copyright 1950 by Random House, Inc. Reprinted by permission.

a very different spirit, by Arnold Bennett), and *The Thread of Gold* (which, as "The Golden Thread," survived as the subtitle for Book II). The fear—or hope—of impending change was destined to be realized, for in the spring of 1858, Dickens and his wife put an end to a long-intolerable domestic situation by arranging a separation. Incidental to that separation was a quarrel between Dickens and his publishers, Bradbury and Evans, and a return on his part to Chapman and Hall, in connection with which disagreement he killed his magazine, *Household Words*, and established a new periodical, *All the Year Round*, whose first issue appeared on April 30, 1859, with the first installment of the new novel in it. Illness during the summer did not make the novelist's task easier, but he managed to keep ahead of the printers, and *A Tale of Two Cities* finished its serial course on November 26, 1859. Between June and December it was also issued, like Dickens's earlier novels, in monthly parts, the last two of which—VII and VIII—appeared together as a double number before Christmas. For the transatlantic rights for one year, an American publisher had meanwhile paid Dickens £1,000.

The book differed notably, both in theme and in technique, from anything that Dickens had hitherto attempted, and of this he himself was well aware. What he had in mind here was, as he told John Forster, *"a picturesque story,* rising in every chapter with characters true to nature, but whom the story should express, more than they should express themselves by dialogue." It was to be a story of incident, in other words, a story for the story's sake; when he had finished it, he "hoped" it was the best story he had written, and, taken as a story, there can be no doubt that it is. "It has greatly moved and excited me in the doing," he told Wilkie Collins, "and Heaven knows I have done my best and believed in it." His letters show how carefully every problem of unity, construction, fore-shadowing, and foreshortening had been considered. Condensation troubled him all along the line, for he was writing a book less than half his standard length, and there was no time to wander down the fascinating bypaths that had such charm for him; every super-fluous word, every nonstructural element had to come out. Aristotle would have approved of it beyond any other of Dickens's novels; for, more clearly than any of the rest, it has a beginning, a middle, and an end.[2]

As all his readers know, "characters true to nature" had not always been Dickens's forte; it is the glory of his eccentrics not that they are true to nature but rather that they surpass it, as, in a very different way, the madonnas of Raphael, which Dickens so passionately admired, surpass nature; for, as James Branch Cabell, once more echoing Aristotle, has reminded us, all romanticists are dedicated to the presentation of life not as it is but as it ought to be. And the expression of character in action rather than in dialogue meant, in effect, for Dickens, learning a brand-new art; for, like Scott, like Shakespeare, he had always realized his characters by permitting them to talk themselves alive, by inventing for each fully-realized personage so distinctive a turn of speech that we hear him forever *as a voice*, and would be sure of his identity if the voice alone came to us over the air waves in the midst of the Gobi Desert. The two methods have little in common except that both are aspects of the dramatic method; for the drama embraces both action and dialogue. But they are different aspects of the dramatic method.

[2] Perhaps only Stryver's interest in Lucie Manette is a nonstructural epi-sode; Jerry Cruncher may, at one stage, seem mere comic relief, but he is very ingeniously taken into the plot before the close.

Comparatively little work has been done on the sources of *A Tale of Two Cities*,[3] and not all of this has been well advised. His most important indebtedness—to Carlyle's *The French Revolution* —Dickens himself avowed in his Preface. He also used Rousseau, the tax tables, and Mercier's *Tableau de Paris*. Dickens greatly admired Carlyle, by whom his own social philosophy was importantly influenced. *The French Revolution* was, indeed, one of his favorite books; he designed his novel as a kind of dramatization of it, and the fact that Carlyle himself had adopted an intensely pictorial style only made his task that much easier. More detailed commentary upon this point would involve a careful comparison between the two works; the last paragraph of Dr. Manette's narrative, for example, comes directly from Carlyle's quotation of a Bastille letter. Edmund Yates declared, on apparently good authority, that Stryver was a portrait of Edwin James, Q.C., whom Dickens saw only once; and Philip Skottowe has considered the case of R. v. de la Motte (1781) as a possible original of Darnay's trial for treason against the British king.[4]

The first performance of Watts Phillips's play, *The Dead Heart* (in which a Frenchman goes to the guillotine to save the son of the woman he loves), on November 10, 1859, while *A Tale of Two Cities* was still running its serial course, occasioned much controversy. Watts Phillips was not indebted to Dickens, for his play is known to have been in existence for some time before it was produced, but there is an unauthenticated story to the effect that it had once been read to the novelist. The so far inconclusive dis-

[3] More has been done since this was written; see, for example, Earle Davis's excellent chapter on the novel in *The Flint and the Flame: The Artistry of Charles Dickens* (University of Missouri Press, 1963).

[4] "The King against Darnay," *Dickensian*, Vol. XXVII (1931), 179–81; cf. also Vol. XLI (1945), 68–74, 129–35; Vol. XLIII (1947), 161.

cussion of this matter[5] has involved both Bulwer's *Zanoni* (already mentioned) and the elder Dumas's *Le Chevalier de la Maison-Rouge* (1847), which Dion Boucicault had adapted into English as *Genevieve; or, The Reign of Terror.* The various works that have been mentioned seem to have little in common outside the element of sacrifice upon the guillotine. Neither does there seem to be any foundation for the statement once made by the illustrator "Phiz" (H. K. Browne) that Dickens shortened *A Tale of Two Cities* after *The Dead Heart* appeared. It was much too late in the day for that.

But it is the book itself which is the thing—not its sources nor its method of production, nor yet what Dickens himself thought about it. We have seen that when he wrote he was trying to do something new, something different. Did he succeed?

There have always been those, even among Dickensians, who have thought that he did not. Gissing did not care for the book, for example. Chesterton entered a divided verdict, complaining among other things that the novelist missed the intellectual side of the Revolution. He did, of course. He missed the intellectual side of everything. He was an intelligent man, but he lived in a highly personal world, and his wisdom, so far as it went, was an intuitive wisdom. He never went so far as mysticism, as Emily Brontë did, and this is his great limitation; his religion, consequently, though completely sincere, was neither faith nor experience, but feeling, sentiment, and morality. Yet Chesterton adds

[5] See John Coleman, "The Truth about 'The Dead Heart' and 'A Tale of Two Cities,'" *New Review*, Vol. I (1889), 542–51, which has recently been rehashed in a queer article by Jack Lindsay, "A Tale of Two Cities," in *Life and Letters*, Vol. LXII (1949), 191–204. A more comprehensive discussion is now that of Carl R. Dolmetsch, "Dickens and *The Dead Heart*," *Dickensian*, Vol. LV (1959), 179–87.

that "in dignity and eloquence," the *Tale* "almost stands alone among the books by Dickens." It pleased Carlyle, and it has been warmly praised by Richard Grant White and by John Drinkwater. The only fair test for the quality of *A Tale of Two Cities* is not whether it is like *Nicholas Nickleby* but whether it achieves successfully what Dickens set out to do. My judgment upon that point I must give frankly for what it is worth. I do not believe that *A Tale of Two Cities* scales the frozen heights of tragic grandeur, as standards in this field have been set by the great tragic writers of the world. But I do believe that it is a fascinating and deeply moving story which must take very high rank indeed among productions of the second rank.

Nor can the book be fairly described as un-Dickensian. It is not like *Nicholas Nickleby*, but it is unmistakably the work of the author of *Nicholas Nickleby*—Jerry Cruncher alone shows that, and Miss Pross, an ugly woman, for once, who is not a shrew— and no other writer could possibly have written it. Nobody else could have described Tellson's Bank in Book II, Chapter 1; nobody else could have so humanized the flies (II, 16) or the material "property" of the shoemaker's bench (II, 19).[6]

Moreover, the moral quality of the book is Dickensian. It is Dickensian in its glorification of love and hatred of cruelty, Dickensian in the sense of destiny which broods over it from the first chapter and contributes notably to the close-knit quality of the fable. Miss Pross wins over Madame Defarge because she grasps her "with the vigorous tenacity of love, always so much stronger

[6] For further comment upon Dickens in this aspect, a kind of folklore quality surviving from primitive man, see Edward Wagenknecht, *Cavalcade of the English Novel* (Holt, 1943), 227, 460. Cf. Priscilla Gibson, "Dickens's Use of Animism," *Nineteenth Century Fiction*, Vol. VII (1953), 283–91.

than hate." Dickens really believed that. As I have pointed out elsewhere,[7] the whole Dickens-Reade-Collins school believed it. We of today, who have lived through horrors they never dreamed of, or which they conceived that the world had done with forever, often find it difficult to believe such things. That is why their sensation-novels are so much more thrilling than ours.

A Tale of Two Cities is one of the most famous of all historical novels, but it is a historical novel in a very special sense. Scott, who set the pattern of historical fiction for the nineteenth century, used famous personages for background in his novels, while the action of the story was carried on by imagined characters whom he might manipulate according to the needs of the plot without being hampered by established biographical fact. Contemporary writers, on the other hand, often make the historical personages themselves their leading dramatis personae. Dickens has no historical personages in the foreground, nor in the background either. In his pages the Revolution is carried on by the Defarges; "it exists," as Andrew Lang perceived, "so to speak, for the story," and even the taking of the Bastille is merely a necessity of the plot. Even before Lang, Forster had pointed out that the most interesting feature of the book in this aspect was the way "in which the domestic life of a few simple private people is . . . knitted and interwoven with the outbreak of a terrible public event."

The method is pictorial as well as dramatic: the revolutionaries huddled around the grindstone are "seen in a moment, as the vision of a drowning man, or of any human creature at any very great pass, could see a world if it were there." The whole book is seen like that; it has a vivid cinematic quality about it. Such a paragraph as this, in Book III, Chapter 3, where Madame Defarge

[7] *Cavalcade of the English Novel,* 235–36.

127

comes to menace Lucie and her child, leaves nothing for the cinema to add:

> The shadow attendant on Madame Defarge and her party seemed to fall so threatening and dark on the child, that her mother instinctively kneeled on the ground beside her, and held her to her breast. The shadow attendant on Madame Defarge and her party seemed then to fall, threatening and dark, on both the mother and the child.

And there is at least one passage, at the close of Book III, Chapter 13, where the setting takes on, for a moment, a cosmic quality:

> The wind is rushing after us, and the clouds are flying after us, and the moon is plunging after us, and the whole wild night is in pursuit of us; but, so far we are pursued by nothing else.

This last passage may seem sophisticated for Dickens, but *A Tale of Two Cities* is far from being primitive in its technique. Somewhere or other, Dickens did almost everything that our *avant-garde* novelists have done; only, he did most of these things unsystematically (perhaps sometimes even un-self-consciously), and they all coexist in him side by side with much that seems to us aesthetically naïve. The procession of faces that passes before Mr. Lorry's mental vision while he is on his way to deliver Dr. Manette (I, 3), the use of the irrelevant in that same Mr. Lorry's supplicatory glance toward the Negro Cupids (I, 4), Lucie's prophetic whim about the footsteps coming into her life (II, 7), young Jerry's wild vision of the coffin running after him (II, 14), and Dr. Manette's memory of bars across the moon—none of this is very far from what we now call "stream-of-consciousness." In Book I, Chapter 3, Darnay's acquittal is reported indirectly, quite in the modern manner; and technically "The Gorgon's Head" (II, 9) has its affinities in technique with the "Time Passes" section of *To the Lighthouse*, by Virginia Woolf.

What, now, of the book in connection with the two shortcomings most commonly charged against Dickens's art—sentimentalism and melodrama?

Personal taste will enter into any verdict that may be entered upon these points—personal taste and the definition of words. I find sentiment but not sentimentality in the touching scene at the end between Carton and the seamstress. I find the description of the death of Darnay's little son (II, 21) exceedingly unpleasant, yet I recognize the existence of historical evidence which shows that children have died in just this way. On the other hand, I find sentimentalism in the bad sense in the third paragraph following, for I do not believe that there is anything in human experience to support the "soft" generalization that Dickens chooses to make. As for the culminating act of the novel, Carton's sacrifice, it undoubtedly appeals to the softer emotions, yet in some aspects Carton may fairly be described as a very unsentimental character. "Hard-boiled" readers of *A Tale of Two Cities* have often declared that Carton did not do so very much after all, for the simple reason that life as he lived it was not much to give up. Up to a point this statement is true, but why should we suppose that either Dickens or Carton himself had overlooked its modicum of truth? By creating the character of Sydney Carton, the "sentimental" Dickens pointed out that some human beings are irreclaimable. For all his "good instincts and good emotions," the Fellow of No Delicacy, though capable of nerving himself to die for love, would find it quite beyond him to live for it.

The chapter in which Miss Pross kills Madame Defarge was

criticized as melodramatic by both Forster and (of all people!) Bulwer-Lytton. Strictly speaking, it is more sensational than melodramatic, for the essential difference between tragedy and melodrama is that in tragedy character determines deeds, while in melodrama we have puppets thrust into sensational situations unconnected in any vital way with their own deeper springs of action. All this Dickens himself clearly perceived:

> I am not clear . . . respecting the canon of fiction which forbids the interposition of accident in such a case as Madame Defarge's death. Where the accident is inseparable from the passion and action of the character; where it is strictly consistent with the entire design, and arises out of some culminating proceeding on the part of the individual which the whole story has led up to; it seems to me to become, as it were, an act of divine justice.

There, again, is the sense of destiny. And if to believe that there is a pattern and a purpose in life (as, in a smaller, more easily perceivable way, there are patterns in plays) be melodramatic, then Dickens will unquestionably have to plead guilty.

Finally, what are the social and political implications of *A Tale of Two Cities*? What attitude did Dickens take up toward the French Revolution? And what, consequently, did he believe about the issues involved?

What T. A. Jackson believed on this point has been set forth in another paper in this collection ("Dickens and the Marxians"). Lenin, as George Orwell reminded us, was wiser than this; he once stalked out of a performance of a play based on *The Cricket on the Hearth* because he was disgusted by its "middle-class sentimentality." From his own point of view he was perfectly right. In *A Tale of Two Cities* Dickens hates both the oppressions of the aristocrats and the sickening cruelties of the revolutionaries. He had a gamin-like contempt for all government and for all the intricacies of the legal mind. The free will of a righteous people, who turn their back upon their sins and purge the social order—this, and this alone, can avert revolution—which, incidentally, is the last thing the Marxian wishes to do. While as for what he thought about dying for a "cause," or "liquidating" individuals to secure its triumph—this, I think, may be safely inferred from the way he handles Madame Defarge and from the rebuke the President administers to Dr. Manette at the end of Book III, Chapter 9. Not for one moment of his existence did Dickens ever believe that human destiny can fulfill itself completely in terms of a historic process. He presented poverty, suffering, death, misfortune, and injustice with an honest and intense sympathy that often mastered his emotions. But through it all he believed in a Divine Ruler who, in the long run, ordered things for the best and assured heavenly reward for the faithful and unfortunate.

Great Expectations[1]

IF I WERE ASKED which novel by Charles Dickens best displayed the rank, heady exuberance of his fecund and inexhaustible genius, pouring itself out recklessly, prodigally, as if the well could never run dry, I should unhesitatingly reply, "*The Pickwick Papers.*" If I were asked which achieved the richest expression of all those qualities of glamour and excitement which we sum up under the term "theater," I should cite *A Tale of Two Cities.* If the inquirer were searching for the book in which he would find the largest quantity of the writer's own great heart and mind in solution in the broth, I should direct him to *David Copperfield.* If, on the other hand, he wanted to study Dickens's mastery of the architectonics of fiction, I should refer him to *Bleak House,* and if he wanted to consider Dickens as a critic of society, I should suggest that he read either *Little Dorrit* or *Our Mutual Friend.* But if you were to ask me where you could expect to find Dickens at his best as an artist, and where you would encounter the perfect blending of the amazingly various yet harmonious qualities which, in their combination, made him one of the great novelists of the world, I should have no hesitation whatever in advising you that you need not look beyond *Great Expectations.*

[1] From the Introduction, by Edward Wagenknecht, to *Great Expectations,* by Charles Dickens. Copyright 1956 by Pocket Books, Inc. Reprinted by permission of Washington Square Press.

Like *David Copperfield*, *Great Expectations* is autobiographical in its method, but now Dickens is using his method much
more carefully; neither is he so much personally involved. Pip is,
in a way, even more of a fool about Estella than David was about
Dora Spenlow. But unlike David, Pip knows that he is a fool; he
understands the girl perfectly—and derives no profit whatever
from his knowledge! This remorseless honesty is one of the
strongest notes in *Great Expectations*, which is one of the most
"modern" among Dickens's novels; in one aspect it looks forward
to such bleak fiction as was coming to England from George
Gissing and other writers. It was because he was so quiveringly
sensitive to the book in this aspect that Bernard Shaw insisted that
it was a profoundly sad book, a deeply disillusioned book, and
this is the truth about it but it is not the whole truth. Not un-
characteristically, Shaw examined with great care only one side of
the 'scutcheon.

For sad as *Great Expectations* is, it is also a kind book and a
mellow book, a book filled with the spirit of forgiveness, of Christian love and forbearance. This world, it says, is a sorry place, but
it is not a hopeless place, for it is a valley of soul-making. It is too
bad that we cannot learn the truth about life without torturing
ourselves as we do, but since we are so stupid, there is no help for
it. There *is* a truth, and it must be learned, and it is worth whatever price we may have to pay for it.

Except for *Hard Times* (always a very special case), *Great
Expectations* was the first Dickens novel in many years that had
not been illustrated, upon its first appearance, with the nervous,
wavering, electrically charged line of "Phiz," in all of whose pictures the personages depicted are as much goblins as human beings.
In comparison, Marcus Stone's pictures seem very matter-of-fact,

even a little drab, and the effect was greatly to accentuate one's impression of the book's modernity. But we must not be misled. Forty-eight is not twenty-four; save for brief episodes, Dickens was never to command the *Pickwick* exuberance again. But the author of *Pickwick* was not dead; neither had he any intention of destroying himself:

> . . . I believe I am exactly what I always was [so he wrote his friend Miss Angela Burdett-Coutts, the great Victorian philanthropist, in the very year *Great Expectations* began]; quite as hopeful, cheerful, and active, as I ever was. I am not so weak or wicked as to visit any small unhappiness of my own, upon the world in which I live. I know very well, it is just as it was. As to my art, I have as great a delight in it as the most enthusiastic of my readers; and the sense of my trust and responsibility in that wise, is always upon me when I take pen in hand. If *I* were soured, I should still try to sweeten the lives and fancies of others, but I am not—not at all.[2]

It was a keen and accurate comment. And in the piece of art which is our concern here, we have a development of "what . . . [he] always was," not a break with it. In *Great Expectations* (to choose but a few examples), we have the popular theater of the early nineteenth century, quite as he had described it in *Nicholas Nickleby* so long ago. Miss Havisham's milieu is as Gothic as anything in *Barnaby Rudge*. Pip's escape from Orlick at the old sluice house is as sensational as the goriest melodrama in *Oliver Twist*. Mr. Wemmick, whose fantastic marriage is used for comic relief just after Provis has been taken—quite in the manner of comic

---

[2] Edgar Johnson, *The Heart of Charles Dickens, As Revealed in His Letters to Angela Burdett-Coutts* . . . (Duell, Sloan and Pearce–Little, Brown, 1952), 370.

relief in the Elizabethan drama—is an eccentric to recall the old days when Dickens's eccentrics had nothing to do but wander in and out of his book, intent upon their silly business (if they had any), and quite unregardful of the needs of the plot (if there was any). Incidentally, Wemmick's fantastic castle takes Dickens back to the dawn not of his writing merely but of his reading, for it is clearly a variant of Commodore Trunnion's house in one of the beloved books of Dickens's boyhood, Smollett's *Peregrine Pickle*. Finally, it is interesting that the author of the *Christmas Books* should have set the opening scenes of his novel—upon the marshes and in the blacksmith's house—at Christmastime, "the worst Christmas in literature," Charles Collins once called it, remembering Pip's sufferings. But as art there is no lack of verve in it for all that, and no lack of tenderness either.

Dickens comes very close to the stream-of-consciousness method in some of these scenes. At the same time they are full of the animism which primitive man freely commanded but which survives today only in children and in those who have kept the hearts of children. Look at the second paragraph of Chapter III and see if it does not cry out for Walt Disney pictures. Then turn to Chapter XI and the horrible description of the decayed wedding cake: ". . . I saw speckled-legged spiders with blotchy bodies running home to it, and running out from it, as if some circumstance of the greatest public importance had just transpired in the spider community." Even horror cannot quite cancel tenderness out! And decay itself is not altogether unbearable with imagination to sweeten it!

As a work of art, *Great Expectations* has long been appreciated; during recent years there has been an increasing tendency to stress its sociological aspects. There is as much snobbery in Pip as in any of Thackeray's heroes. It is undeniable that the boy belongs to what some people now find it interesting to call the proletariat; it is also true that he is painfully class-conscious. Mr. Jaggers, as his endless hand-washing shows, is well aware that his business is a pretty dirty business. Whether Dickens meant all this to be taken so sociologically as we are inclined to do is a question. Mr. Jaggers has at least some of his roots in the novelist's life-long mistrust of everything connected with the law, and Pip's principal source of distress about Provis is not that he is a convict merely, but rather Pip's feeling that the disappearance of the imagined tie with Miss Havisham weakens his chances with Estella. The sociological note may be there for all that, and there is no harm in sounding it, so long as it is not permitted to drown out the other notes. Like all good novels, *Great Expectations* is a story about *people*, and Dickens saw people as spiritual beings; they might be grievously oppressed by political institutions and heavily handicapped by economic maladjustments but neither politics nor economics could be the making of them. Joe Gargery is a figure of fun, but he is also a saint, and he tests those who come near him for gold and for alloy, much as Jim does in *Huckleberry Finn*. When the novel opens Joe is ignorant of what can be learned from books, and he remains ignorant to the end, for he is incapable of book learning, but he is rich in the wisdom of the understanding heart. This is precisely the wisdom which the much more intelligent Pip must painfully spell out for himself, and as he does so there are times when he strains our sympathy greatly. But the basic reason for this is that we know in our hearts that we are much more like him than we are like Joe.

"Immortal Memory"

A TOAST AT THE DICKENS FELLOWSHIP CONFERENCE DINNER
AT PARKER HOUSE, BOSTON, MASS., ON JUNE 9, 1962

Mr. Chairman and Fellow Dickensians:

I wonder if Mr. Peyrouton knows just how much he did to bolster my ego by asking me to give the toast to the Immortal Memory tonight. It happens that, forty-five years ago next Thursday night, in Oak Park, Illinois, I graduated from high school. I was valedictorian of the class; the class prophet was a boy named Ernest Hemingway. Because of my well-known indifference to all forms of athletic sports I appeared in his class prophecy as a famous baseball player. On this basis I have always claimed that I was one of the first Hemingway characters. Frederic Henry, Catherine Barkley, Lady Brett Ashley, Robert Jordan—I got in ahead of them all! And now, as I stand here tonight, I can't help remembering the many distinguished men and women who have stood where I stand at Conference banquets of the past, and particularly I cannot but remember that not so many years ago, in London, I was preceded in my present capacity by no less a personage than Mr. Chaplin, himself surely the greatest inheritor of the Dickens tradition. It really makes me feel as if here tonight I were inheriting one of Chaplin's roles! If I should stay around for another forty-five years—and I can certainly see no reason why I should not—who can dare to say what I might by that time achieve?

One of the most suggestive passages I know in recent Dickens criticism occurs in the chapter on *Oliver Twist* in J. Hillis Miller's *Charles Dickens: The World of His Novels.* As Dickens first wrote it, Bill Sikes was one of those "insensible and callous natures that do become, at last, utterly and *irredeemably* bad." But "in the version of the preface for the Charles Dickens Edition of 1856 this became 'utterly and *incurably* bad,' evidently to remove the theological implication of 'irredeemably.' Dickens," as Professor Miller sees it, "did not want to deny God's power to redeem even those who are apparently hopelessly evil."

This is the kind of self-revelation on the part of an author that is of particular value to a biographer. When a man *tells* you what he believes, he leaves his statement open to discount for various reasons. But when he makes such a change as this in what he himself has written, you see what is going on in his own heart. There is no question now of bearing a testimony, and there is certainly no thought of being on dress parade.

I believe that the attitude toward human nature suggested in this passage goes far toward explaining the character of Dickens's fiction, his charm, and the sureness of his hold upon his readers so long after most of his contemporaries have lost theirs. I believe, too, that it takes on an added interest from being not merely the expression of a kindly man's soft-hearted (or soft-headed) confidence in his own kind: it is always much too easy for such statements to shade off into mere sentimentality. Dickens builds his faith in mankind upon the one sure foundation—the religious foundation. He assumes that man is made in the image of God. With God's life in him he can never be quite irredeemable. However deep the godliness within may be buried, however he may have soiled and violated it, there will still be that which "a man may waste, desecrate, never quite lose." For Dickens as for Browning, this something had an otherworldly origin. It is not necessary to stop here to inquire what would be his attitude toward those modern heresies in religion which try to find the sense of the sacred in human nature itself. He was not a gifted theologian, but we may be sure he would perceive at once that this is merely a new form of idolatry, and that whoever should attempt to build his life upon such a faith would rest his weight on the thinnest, most treacherous reed of them all.

As Dickens grew older, he tended increasingly to lose faith in the English government—and in all government, for that matter —but, for the most part, he retained his faith in mankind. "My faith in the people governing," he said, "is on the whole infinitesimal; my faith in The People governed, is, on the whole illimitable."

There are exceptions, to be sure. There are evil men and women in Dickens's last novels, and their evil is the more impressive because he no longer conceives them in the somewhat melodramatic terms which, at the beginning of his career, he had employed to set forth such creatures as Fagin. In life he always opposed the tendency to allow criminals to pose as heroes, and one of the reasons he opposed capital punishment was that he believed it martyrizes the criminal and invests him with a horrible romantic glow which he would otherwise not possess. He believed that criminals are frequently without conscience altogether and that often they struggle toward crime as diligently as decent people struggle away from it. Dickens was a hard man as well as a kind one, and for all the charges of sentimentality that have been leveled against him, I know nothing more unsentimental in all literature than what the Chalons landlady says in *Little Dorrit* of those "people (men and women both, unfortunately) who have no good in them—none." She believes "that there are people whom it is necessary to detest without compromise. That there are people who must be dealt with as enemies of the human race. That there are people who have no human heart, and who must be crushed like savage beasts and cleared out of the way."

> *Do I contradict myself?* [asks Whitman].
> *Very well then I contradict myself.*
> *(I am large, I contain multitudes).*

"A foolish consistency," said Emerson, "is the hobgoblin of small minds." Was Dickens, then, inconsistent in his attitude toward human nature? Well, if he was, we ought not to be greatly surprised, for few men have ever been anything else. But even the exploration of an inconsistency may shed considerable light on the man who entertains it.

The fundamental reason why it is difficult or impossible to be entirely consistent in one's attitude toward human nature is of course the fact that human nature is in itself inconsistent. Man is an animal—who has somehow developed a soul. He alone among created things has a conscience, and he alone is capable of sin. I read somewhere the other day about a man who considered great affection for animals on the part of a human being an immoral and unamiable trait: people who love animals, he said, do not love human beings. I do not believe that this is true. It was not true of Dickens, for example. But even if I thought it was, I should not feel any obligation to give the animals up. It is high time man got it through his thick skull that he is not the sole evidence of the

Creator's power, and that he shares this earth with a vast variety of other creatures, all of whom have their rights as he has his, and whose rights are sacred in the eyes of God even when he chooses (as he generally does) to disregard them. I am told that one of our hellish nuclear tests in the Pacific the other day blinded rabbits nearly 300 miles away, and I say deliberately and quite seriously that I pray that the souls of these wronged and injured beasts may rise in the Judgment to damn all those who were responsible for this atrocity. We should not, I fancy, regard Shakespeare as the greatest of all English writers if no opinion but Shakespeare's had ever been recorded on the matter. It is a humiliating thing for *homo sapiens* to be obliged to reflect that the universally-accepted notion that man is the king and crown of creation is an opinion which is peculiar to himself. None of the rest of creation has ever been polled on the matter.

Chesterton once pointed out that Dickens's delighted relish of eccentricity was the relish of a normal man: if you are off center yourself then the eccentric becomes your norm. I said a moment ago that a kindly, loving attitude toward human nature can avoid the bogs of sentimentality only when it is grounded firmly in religious faith: man is a fallen creature, to whose sinfulness there is almost no limit, yet at the same time man is a fallen creature for whose redemption God was willing to die. Now I would not say that Dickens was never sentimental. What I would say is that when Dickens did choose to be sentimental, he sentimentalized the kind of creature that a normal, healthy, sensible man might be expected to sentimentalize, that he could hardly be a normal, healthy, sensible man without sentimentalizing. There is a whole school of modern fiction in which "Mom" is a dastardly villainess, warping her children's lives, but the "Madame" at the neighborhood brothel is a glorious rich Earth Mother with a Heart of Gold, upon whose capacious and all-loving bosom the hero comes at last to rest. Let us not forget that even so intelligent a writer as Van Wyck Brooks once published a book in which Mark Twain's mother was represented as having warped his life and prevented him from attaining his full stature as an artist because when he left home as a youngster she made him promise to be a good boy, and let us also remember the far more appalling fact that though the book in which the accusation was made has never been accepted by a single Mark Twain specialist, it still maintains a surprising hold over people who prefer theories about literature to literature. John Steinbeck sentimentalizes tramps and idiots; in such books as *Of Mice and Men* and *Cannery Row* the sweet simplicities of the Friendship Village School turn to a glorification of mindlessness. Ernest Hemingway sentimentalized alcoholics, perverts, and warped souls in general. In *An American Tragedy* Theodore Dreiser sentimentalized a youthful murderer because life had played a dirty trick on him by causing him to be born in a milieu in which he had to work for a living instead of devoting all his time to party-going. I am not saying that these books have no value. I am not saying that none of the people in them are worthy of sympathy. I am saying that they wallow at times in a sentimentality to which neither Charles Dickens nor Samuel Richardson (nor, for that matter, Kate Douglas Wiggin nor Eleanor H. Porter) ever descended. Dickens sentimentalized Paul Dombey and Little Nell. He tended, I fear, to sentimentalize women in general, when they were young and attractive, that is. (When they were not, he always inclined, in his fiction at least, to make ogres of them.) He paid a heavy price for this, certainly as an artist and possibly as a man, and it may be that it was a sign of emotional immaturity in him that he should have done it. But I think you will be disposed to grant, if you are honest, that if you are going to be sentimental about anybody or anything, it is healthier to be sentimental about Little Nell—or, for that matter, Dora Spenlow—than it is to be sentimental about some of the creatures that rouse sympathy most quickly and surely in many contemporary writers. I do not know whether there ever was a girl who was quite such an ideal creature as Little Nell; I have never been such a girl myself, and I cannot tell. But I should not care much for any *young* man who could not *believe* in such a girl. As for Dora Spenlow, I should hope, for his sake, that the young man would not take her quite at face value as David did, but I do not really love David less for having done so, though I must add that I should not have much respect for an older man who made the same mistake. But about that Dickens perfectly agreed, and that is why Dora had to die. We all remember what happened when *his* Dora Spenlow, Maria Beadnell, who did not die, tried coming back into his life as Mrs. Winter, and forthwith found herself somewhat heartlessly transformed into Flora Finching.

I was much amused the other day, in reading some notes written by the English music critic, Desmond Shawe-Taylor, to accompany an Angel reissue of some John McCormack records on Long Play, to learn that the printed text of "The Star of the County Down" contains the lines:

And I'll try sheep's eyes and deludtherin' lies
On the heart of the nut-brown Rose.

You will not hear McCormack sing these lines. This was not his notion of how a gallant Irish lover behaves. Instead he sings:

With me shoes shone bright and me hat cock'd right
For a smile from the nut-brown Rose.

And I could not help remembering that when McCormack recorded "Little Wooden Head" from Disney's *Pinocchio* he
altered the song as it had been sung in the film so as to omit mention of a certain portion of the puppet's anatomy which did not
seem to him a lyrical subject. McCormack has been dead now for
nearly seventeen years, and during this period we have gone far
toward establishing the principle that the stage is a place where
you go when you want to dump garbage. Devoted theatergoer that
he was, I wonder what he would say if he knew what has been
inflicted upon us during these years.

What Dickens would say we know. He objected to Wilkie
Collins's dramatization of *Armadale* on the ground that the
characters were too wicked for anybody to be interested in. "You
could only carry those situations," he wrote, "*by the help of interest
in some innocent young person whom they placed in peril, and that
person a young woman.*" And though he defended Charles Reade's
Griffith Gaunt as "the work of a highly accomplished writer and
a good man," he admitted that he found certain situations in it
"extremely coarse and disagreeable," and said that he would not
have passed them as editor because "what was pure to an artist
might be impurely suggestive to inferior minds (of which there
must necessarily be many among a large mass of readers)."

Well, perhaps it is not necessary to go quite as far as that.
Light shines most brightly against a background of darkness, and
nobody in this day and age wants to deny artists the privilege of
portraying the contrast. For that matter, nobody in this day and
age wants to draw the line between the permissible and the non-

permissible in art quite where the Victorians drew it. But the first of the two statements I have just quoted is the more interesting, and how much need we have of it we never realize quite so clearly as when we hear somebody say that all the most interesting people in literature are more or less rascals and all the saints are bores. This, surely, is a statement which has more autobiographical than critical value. Of course saints are dull in literature when they are portrayed dully, that is to say when they are portrayed in a milk-and-water fashion by a writer who does not understand sainthood and is incapable of setting it forth upon its own terms. Are Joan of Arc and Francis of Assisi bores? Is Judas more interesting than Christ in the Passion drama? The plain truth of the matter is that sinners are not very interesting in literature except as they hold our sympathy through our consciousness of the good in them which their sins undercut and make of no avail. *Macbeth* is the greatest villain-hero play ever written, for the simple reason that Shakespeare convinces us at the outset that Macbeth was a great man, with a great capacity for goodness, who took the wrong turning. *Richard III*, though much less great, holds our interest in large part because the playwright very skillfully directs our attention away from the merely evil qualities in Richard's nature to his wit, his energy, his insight into human nature, and his executive skill— qualities amoral in themselves, immoral in the use which Richard makes of them, and most suggestive of all in their unused potential. Shakespeare knew this. Dickens knew it. Every writer of any reputation at all knows it, with the possible exception of Mr. Mickey Spillane and the critics who ought to confine themselves to an exclusive diet of his wares.

I have heard the preoccupation of modern artists with filth and confusion defended upon the ground that an artist must mirror the age in which he lives. I should have said that it is the function of an artist to clarify and to redeem the age in which he lives. I have heard that we must have perverts and idiots upon the stage because we have them in life. But we are not *all* perverts and idiots in life—thank you!—and we resent your assumption that normal people are not interesting enough to write about. And if we were, then there would be all the more good reason why art should give us something that life cannot afford. Art is not life, and life is not art. If life could satisfy all our needs at first hand, what need should we have of art? And if what art offers falls far *below* the level of life, what function can it serve but to degrade us?

Moreover, though art is not life, it is based on life; if it does not mirror the way we live, it does mirror our taste and our thinking. Oscar Wilde was quite right when he declared that life imitates art quite as much as art imitates life. Thought is creative, and the image of itself which one age creates upon the stage may well find itself during the next generation in the world, which is but a larger stage. Of course we should not shrink from ugliness and veil our eyes from evil in so far as our contacts and our contemplation can tend to redeem ugliness and cure evil. But to make a cult of ugliness and evil and to devote one's exclusive attention to them is something else again. A surgeon spends a good deal of his working time looking at diseased tissues, but he looks at them for the purpose of destroying them; once he should find himself more attracted to the diseased tissues than the healthy ones, then Othello's occupation would be gone indeed. Nor have I ever heard of a successful surgeon who felt it necessary to hang the walls of his dining room with photographs of operations. Mr. Tennessee Williams, one of our most gifted and successful specialists in the abnormal and the obscene, has recently made the statement that he has now finished with this sort of thing in his art. He has said what he has to say about it—and God knows I don't see how he could say anything more than he has said!—and from now on he is going to be constructive. It will be interesting to see if this promise is kept. I hope very much that it may be, but I do not really believe that it will. I fear Mr. Williams will find that his creative imagination cannot be stimulated by the normal and the constructive.

Dickens had the dramatic imagination as much as it was ever possessed by a writer who did not write significantly for the stage: he tells us that as soon as the idea for *A Tale of Two Cities* came to him, he became anxious "to embody it in my own person." The actor gives us himself along with the character he plays; instead of being lost in his rôle, he enlarges it; and it is no accident that Dickens should give us himself along with his books as few novelists have done it. He did not exactly write by dramatizing his own personality as Byron and Mark Twain did, as, in a very different way, Milton did, and this is fortunate, for if he had done so he could never have commanded the range which, as it is, he knows; yet every line of dialogue he wrote, every sentence in which the story moves forward, every descriptive passage even, is steeped in a personality and a point of view which was Charles Dickens and nobody else on earth. He once declared that he was not sure whether it was his gift or his infirmity to view all life, as he did, from an angle which, he was well aware, differed in important aspects from that of other people. It was, of course, both, and it is very fortunate for us that, giving himself to us, as he did, in this highly dramatic way, the quality of the personality with which the drink was spiked should have been such a wholesome personality as it was. Otherwise Dickens would have been as great a force for corruption as, under existent circumstances, he has been a force for good.

147

Like Melville, he knew that a work of fiction is a kind of theater between covers; men go to it, as they go to the theater, for glamour; at the same time, they go to it for truth; from it they expect, in a sense, "more reality than real life itself can show." "It is with fiction as with religion," Melville concludes; "it should present another world, and yet one to which we feel the tie."

Dickens would not have formulated the matter, perhaps, in quite those terms, but basically he would have agreed. The nature of his imagination was dramatic; he *believed*, too, in the drama and in the theater; he sympathized with those aspects and tendencies in human character which gravitate toward the theater. "The close of the story is unnecessarily painful," he writes to one contributor to his journal. Nor could he perceive any reason why the English, "the hardest-worked people on whom the sun shines," should, "in their wretched intervals of pleasure," be expected to give their attention to any work of art which did not amuse them. And simple and childlike as he was in his own religious faith, reverent as he always was toward the manifestation of religious faith in general, he parts company with any religionist at the precise point where religion is swallowed up in gloom. Who, for example, ever penned a more scorching denunciation than this of the Shakers and, by implication, of all gloomy, ascetic religion?

I so abhor, and from my soul detest that bad spirit, no matter by what class or sect it may be entertained, that would strip life of its healthful graces, rob youth of its innocent pleasures, pluck from maturity and age their pleasant ornaments, and make existence but a narrow path towards the grave: that odious spirit which, if it could have had full scope and sway upon the earth, must have blasted and made barren the imagination of the greatest men, and left them, in their power of raising up enduring images before their fellow-creatures yet unborn, no better than the beasts; that, in these very broad-brimmed hats and very sombre coats—in stiff-necked, solemn-visaged piety, in short, no matter what its garb, whether it have cropped hair as in a Shaker village, or long nails as in a Hindoo temple—I recognise the worst among the enemies of Heaven and Earth, who turn the water at the marriage feasts of this poor world, not into wine, but gall. And if there must be people vowed to crush the harmless fancies and the love of inno-cent delights and gaieties, which are a part of human nature: as much a part of it as any other love or hope that is our common portion: let them, for me, stand openly revealed among the ribald and licentious; the very idiots know that they are not on the im-mortal road, and will despise them, and avoid them readily.

If you had to give up all Dickens's novels except one, which would you retain? I do not see how I could get along without *David Copperfield*. But then if I kept *Copperfield*, what would I do without *Pickwick*, or even more without *Great Expectations?* We used to assume that Dickens changed the original ending of *Great Expectations* out of consideration for the wishes of his pub-lic, as presented to him by Bulwer-Lytton; I think this view mis-taken. I do not believe that Dickens would have changed the original ending unless Bulwer had convinced him that he was right. It was the original ending of *Great Expectations* that was wrong, for Dickens's hand had faltered. He changed it because he was a big enough man to realize that he had been wrong, and the revised ending is right.

In what I have to say upon this subject I am much indebted to an article by my friend Professor Ernest Boll of the University of Pennsylvania, published some years ago in the London *Times Literary Supplement*.[1] What he had to say I state in my own words, and I do not at this time, without recourse to his text, know how much is Wagenknecht and how much is Boll. But it now seems to me so obvious that, despite my grateful indebtedness to Professor Boll, I think I was very stupid not to have perceived all this without him, and I can only comfort myself by reflecting that I shared my stupidity with John Forster, Bernard Shaw, and a great many other wise people, but not Ernest Boll—nor Charles Dickens. I think too that this final disposition of the problem of *Great Expectations* illustrates, perhaps more convincingly than anything else I could say, some of the truths about Charles Dickens which I have tried to present to you tonight, and with it, for that reason, I bring my remarks to a close.

Those who reject the revised ending of *Great Expectations* usually assume that it is a happy "boy gets girl" ending. It has not been prepared for, they argue, and therefore it is wrong. Moreover, Estella would certainly make Pip thoroughly miserable. When did she ever do anything else?

But the revised ending of *Great Expectations* is not that kind of an ending at all. Pip comes to Estella at last as a kind of second choice, after he has missed out with Biddy. And the girl he marries is not quite the girl who lived with Miss Havisham so long ago, and of whom her corrupter-benefactress cried, when she had got her eyes opened at last, "I stole her heart away and put ice in its place." And again: " 'What have I done? What have I done?' And so again, twenty, fifty times over, What had she done?" Estella paid a heavy price for her conditioning at Miss Havisham's hands.

[1] August 15, 1935, p. 513. During recent years a number of other writers on Dickens have independently arrived at Boll's view.

Since we last saw her, she has gone through the waters of tribulation indeed. Is it necessary to assume that she is quite a fool, that she has learned nothing from these experiences?

Bernard Shaw thought *Great Expectations* a profoundly sad book. It is a sad book only in the sense that it faces the facts of the human condition. It is also a mellow book, a book filled with the spirit of forgiveness, of Christian love and forbearance. Its mood is a mood of reconciliation. Pip is reconciled to Miss Havisham and to the convict. In a somewhat comic way, which would seem heartless if she had not hitherto been such a comic termagant, he is even reconciled to his sister Mrs. Gargery. Only old Orlick is at last left out; he alone can be nominated as one of the Chalons landlady's "enemies of the human race," "people who have no human heart" —for salvation is not universal in the Dickens world, nor in that of the New Testament. But Estella was no Orlick, and it is hard to see why she should be excluded.

And now, ladies and gentlemen, may I ask you to join with me in drinking the toast to "The Immortal Memory of Charles Dickens."

Index

CD indicates Charles Dickens
ET indicates Ellen Ternan
EW indicates Edward Wagenknecht
HWL indicates Henry Wadsworth Longfellow

Drinkwater, John: 126
Dumas, Alexandre: 125
DuCann, C. G. L.: 14, 40
Duffield, Howard: 119

Eliot, George: 42, 112
Ellis, Havelock: 116
Elsna, Hebe: 45
Emerson, Ralph Waldo: 140

Fadiman, Clifton: 12, 25
Fagin, Bob: 20
Fechter, Charles, CD's admiration for and friendship with: 92–94
Felton, Cornelius C.: 74–75, 76, 78
Field, Kate: 92
Fielding, Kenneth J.: 5, 16
Fields, James T.: 85, 87, 92–93
Fields, Annie Adams (Mrs. James T.): on CD and HWL, 85–86; on CD and Fechter, 92–93
Forster, John: 12, 45–46, 52, 55, 57–58, 63, 77, 78, 79, 84, 86–89, 104, 112, 122, 127, 130, 150

Gissing, George: 116, 125
Glasgow, Ellen, her admiration for CD and imitation of *Great Expectations*: 95–98
Goldring, Martha: 18
Gordan, John D.: 32, 37
Greene, George Washington: 82
Greenleaf, Mary Longfellow (Mrs. James): 71
Grubb, Gerald G.: on Ada Nisbet, 32–33; references to, 13, 36, 43

Hardman, Sir William: 29–31

on CD's separation from his wife, 86–87; on his death, 87–88; on Forster's *Life*, 87–89; *see also entries under* Dickens, Charles
Longfellow, Samuel: 71–73, 83–84

Mackintosh, Mary Appleton (Mrs. Robert): 86, 87
Mansfield, Katherine, and CD: *see under* Dickens, Charles
Mark Twain (Samuel Langhorne Clemens): 22, 110, 119, 136, 142, 147
Masters, Edgar Lee: 110
Marxian criticism of CD: 109–13
Maugham, W. Somerset: 25; on CD and ET, 10–11; on Georgina Hogarth, 11
McCormack, John: 143–44
Melville, Herman: 148
Mill, John Stuart: 63–64
Miller, J. Hillis: 138
Milton, John: 48, 147
Monroe, Marilyn: 25

Nisbet, Ada: 13, 24–25, 28, 37, 40, 47; chides EW for ignoring *TLS* statement by Bernard Shaw, 21; why she wrote *Dickens and Ellen Ternan*, 25; *Dickens and Ellen Ternan* considered, new material in, 32–33; fails to prove her case, 33–34; misunderstands EW's purpose, 34–35; alleges considerations irrelevant to her criticism of EW, 35–36
Norton, Andrews: 74
Norton, Charles Eliot: 74
Nuclear testing: 141

Orczy, Baroness: 121
Orwell, George: 130

Trollope, T. A.: 13, 27–28

Van Amerongen, J. B., on CD's dramatic method: 107

Wagenknecht, Edward: enters CD–ET controversy, 13; Nisbet on,
    21–22, 25; Aylmer on, 25; Hudson on, 26–31; Nisbet misses
    purpose of, 34–36
Ward, Sam: 16
Waugh, Arthur: 16
Wharton, Edith: 115, 116
Wheeler, Jane: 47
Whiffen, Mrs. Thomas: 35
Whipple, E. P.: 63–64
White, Richard Grant: 126
Whitman, Walt: 140
Whittier, John Greenleaf: 42–43
Wiggin, Kate Douglas: 142
Wilde, Oscar: 146
Williams, Tennessee: 146–47
Wills, W. H.: 29
Wilson, Edmund: 25; his critical irresponsibility, 9–10, 116–17; his
    foreword to Nisbet, 32, 33–34; his "Dickens: The Two
    Scrooges," 114–21; his incompetent handling of the CD–ET
    problem, 118–19; ignores Victorian novel backgrounds, 118;
    handicapped by Freudian methods, 119
Winter, William: 65, 92
Woolf, Virginia: 129
Wright, Thomas: 10, 22–23, 26, 40, 47; his charges against CD and
    ET, 7–8, 9, 15–21; his *Daily Express* article, 7; his *Life of
    Charles Dickens*, 7; his *Autobiography*, 18–19

Yates, Edmund: 124

Dickens and the Scandalmongers has been set on the Linotype in eleven and one-half point Caslon Old Face with three points of spacing between the lines. Foundry Caslon Roman and Italic has been used for display. This book has been printed on paper designed for an effective life of at least three hundred years.

UNIVERSITY OF OKLAHOMA PRESS

NORMAN